LOOKING OUT, LOOKING IN

By E. A. Markham

E. A. MARKHAM

Looking Out,
Looking In

NEW AND SELECTED POEMS

ANVIL PRESS POETRY

Published in 2009
by Anvil Press Poetry Ltd
Neptune House 70 Royal Hill London SE10 8RF
www.anvilpresspoetry.com

ISBN 978 0 85646 414 0

This book is published
with financial assistance from
Arts Council England

A catalogue record for this book
is available from the British Library

Designed and set in Monotype Bulmer by Anvil
Printed and bound in England
by Cromwell Press Group
Trowbridge, Wiltshire

Contents

PART TWO: from *Human Rites*, 1984

PART THREE: from *Living in Disguise*, 1986

PART FOUR: from *Towards the End of a Century*, 1989

ACKNOWLEDGEMENTS

Some of the 'new' poems have appeared in the following publications: *Agenda*, *Ambit*, *Blinking Eye Website*, *The British Council Newsletter* (Ireland), *London Magazine*, *Magma*, *Matter 2*, *The North*, *P.N Review*, *Poetry Review*, *The Rialto*, *The TLS*, *The Trinidad & Tobago Review*, *Wasafiri* and in the anthologies *Caribbean Quarterly* (the John Figueroa memorial issue) and *A Company of Poets* (Hearing Eye, 2003). 'The Thing Not Said' was displayed as a 'Poem on the Underground' in 2006.

John Lewis & Co. was published as an Anvil booklet in 2003.

In 2005, the Poetry Archive (London) recorded 20 of these poems and produced a CD, *E. A. Markham: Reading From His Poems* (www.poetryarchive.org).

– E. A. M.

The publisher thanks Arc Publications for permission to include the poems from *Letter from Ulster & The Hugo Poems*, first published by Littlewood Arc in 1993.

Preface

E. A. ('Archie') Markham died at Easter 2008 in Paris, his home since retiring in 2005 from the Creative Writing department at Sheffield Hallam University. He had sent the Contents list and most of the new poems for this collection a couple of months earlier, and we were to meet and make final adjustments to it when he next visited England.

Since this meeting could not take place, we are publishing the collection largely unaltered and as he had planned it, with the addition of notes compiled from those in earlier collections. He had consulted Mimi Khalvati at various stages while putting the collection together and I am most grateful for her help and advice in preparing the book for press.

By 'largely' I mean that there are some details we cannot be certain about. He told us, for example, that two poems were missing from the collection as he sent it. They were from the group 'A Family Epic': one entitled 'Something Remembered', which was to have gone after 'Family Matters', and the second called 'Family Graves', to finish the group after 'Little Miracles'. However, the group here is numbered as it was in his typescript, so the two extra poems would have been late additions.

Also missing was 'Woman on the Verandah, Reflects'; I have used a typescript from May 2004 with no certainty that it is the final version. Likewise I am unsure that the prose text 'Why Do You Write?' is his latest version: the text here is from our files and is dated June 2002.

There are other anomalies and uncertainties which may be worth noting. The group of three poems entitled 'Against War' – so named in the body of his typescript, and referred to by him as such in correspondence – was given as 'Against the War' in his Contents list. It is a nice distinction and a close editorial call.

He had stated that two poems from the 'West Indian Myths' sequence, numbers 3 and 4, were to have new last lines, but we do not have them. The selection from *Living in Disguise* – shorter than might be expected because he had decided not to include any poems written in his wonderful *personae* of Sally Goodman and Paul St Vincent – opens here with six haiku, where the book had only the first two: the other four are from his next collection, *Towards the End of a Century*. He had indicated that '8 from various books' were to go here, which leaves two unaccounted for.

Since he had also stated an intention to add some poems from two collections which he felt he had under-represented, *Misapprehensions* and *A Rough Climate*, Mimi Khalvati and I have added a number of poems from them, well aware that they are unlikely to be the ones which he himself would have picked. These additions are marked with an asterisk in the Contents.

Archie's unexpected early death deprived us of a writer in full flow. His energy and productivity were extraordinary. Readers of his poetry who have not yet discovered his prose books – two late collections of stories (one of them posthumous) and the memoir make a good start – have a treat in store.

As his main poetry publisher for more than two decades I should like to record my pleasure not only in his writing – which displays an invigorating kind of intelligence, given to thinking and arguing in a way that seems to me distinctive and original – but also in all my contact, from office to cricket ground, with a most engaging and inspiriting friend and ally.

PETER JAY

1

New Poems

The Three of Us

He calls her generous.
'Generous!' shrieks the husband.
'How can he call her that:
I've been married to the woman
for X years, and "generous"
has never been her synonym.'

He calls her generous,
the lover, suggesting trysts
in places where the in-set
play. They rendezvous some way
from an Islington of Pop Art,
chamber music, poems.

'Punitive,' says the husband,
that curl and set of the mouth.
And the language! He's beginning
to warm to the lingo:
you go with the flow, you've been
beaten at school, you take the rough

with the rough. 'I'll take punitive'.
Enter third party. That's me,
hovering between generous &
punitive. I can swing this way
or that. I'm a TA Volunteer;
I read Keats. I'm balanced.

The Story of a Revolution

Grandmother is reading Ruskin's *Seven Lamps of Architecture.*
The year is 1956 in Coderington, St. Caesare
And the Revolution is forty years off, so scholars argue
Over how much reading grandmother has got through in the years
Since she died, a detail well worth mention, as when it comes
The Revolution will be disguised as natural phenomena
And presented as hurricane and volcano; and the name Krueger,
Appearing in records of the time, will be an error.

So grandmother, alive and reading her book, can be allowed
To be distracted a little by whispers about Krueger.
Pewter, the boy, destined for England, sixteen years old, let's say,
Buys a sugar-cake at Krueger's shop: there's no such shop, of course.
When he describes it, it's Mr Lee's shop. What, grandmother asks,
Has Krueger done with Mr Lee? Nobody knows: why then
Aren't they curious? Nellie, the maid, is reading those servants' parts
In Molière that make you hopeful. Pewter is reading Hakluyt.

There's little thought now of the revolution that didn't happen.
Though Krueger makes an appearance out of context, as a comic;
And Miss Na and Tan Tan and Uncle Mike are given more credit
For having lived in those times. And the boy, Pewter, tells the story
Of early days in England unable to talk to workmates
About Hakluyt, because either Hakluyt or Pewter's accent
Was unfamiliar. So here's Krueger in costume, gun in hand.
I am Krueger, he says. No discussion. No nonsense. Chop chop.

My Mother's Country

It was evening and the fire had stopped smoking in the grate.
We were watching television, one of those programmes that
    mother & children
could view together; and the knock at the door unnerved us as
    it was late;
mother wondered if we were beginning to fall into bad habits.
And, in truth, we were startled by a man at the door dressed to
    impress the family.
He spoke good English: the message, he said, for the mother of
    the house,
is from the king. Though unexpected this was something subtly
    understood;
and the sitting-room was rearranged for the meeting.

The mother must know, the messenger said, that war had been
    declared
in her name. The family, always understated, managed to take it
    in their stride:
would this make up for disappointments suffered earlier in the
    country?
But we must thank the king: win or lose our name would be in
    the history books
just when we were beginning to feel undervalued. Mother could
    start
by taking an interest in tactics and manoeuvres, and in the nature
    of weaponry.
But for now the questions can wait; treat it as just another thing
    that happened;
and make up the sofa bed for the boy who needs to sleep.

Mother will not let this opportunity slip. As a woman head of
    house
her thinking is strategic: one son has already written a play,

the daughter is leaf-perfect in botany, the king's nod is no accident.
The family will rehearse the national debates here in this house
and allocate to the other boy the dissenters' role heading riots in
    the street,
but exile him before the civil war becomes history. She will keep
    he divines sweet
because of her background; and bring her own husband back from
    abroad
to be in charge of the new pavilion, or the horses.

The following day we got out the atlas and a map to see what
    territory
would be taken in our name: if a brother was late for work
and another for school, the excuses could be passed off as
    diplomacy.
The family were curious about the people they'd inherit: what
    language
did they speak in that place, was it this or that shape on the map,
    how
to pronounce it in public? Mother is working on a statement about
    the dead
and wounded; alas, before arts and religion could flourish again
    there.
And the king: if he didn't deliver this time, what then would be
    the plan?

Belief

I believe in hell, of course
because my neighbour comes from there:
the horns are tired today and hang
like tresses from a too-white face;
the lipstick red is scary;
and the hoofs are well-disguised
in carpet-slippers: she's a dancer
at the *Moulin Rouge* up the hill.

I stage-whisper my concern
to house-strangers at the bottom of the lift
that this new athlete on the sixth floor
is heavy as our *cantatrice* down below
is light: she can't tell heel from toe.
But yes, she comes in at 2.30
in the morning and dismounts;
and the flat vibrates: how does she fit the beast
into the lift? No wonder, released,
it stamps and rages above my head
demanding to be let out.
Sleep's not the issue now, more
the physics of a Paris ceiling. Without
tranquilliser gun or tourist's courage
I climb the stairs in the night, armed
with Plan B, so I could at least demand
respect for animals in the house.

And here she comes, wary-eyed
like a victim, small & ready to attack:
soft-porn curtain fingered back
from the face to unsteady me, blood
on the lips licked clean, the hoofs
slippered again like feet. She listens,
she struggles to comprehend; till the eyes

glint on a flaw in the argument: how is it,
they seem to say – and the neighbour begins
to change into something familiar –
that hell is a flat *above* your own?

Against War: Three Poems

War

They read together, he reads to her;
so, how's that for doing your own thing, then!
She reminds him he's now low on *Betagan, Xalatan.*

The planes and boats bring other cargo,
soldiers and things that soldiers need;
this is like riches, soon there'll be everything.

The riots won't last; they must bury their dead;
things are returning, daily, to normal.
Sorry about the betagan; *she'll* read to him.

A Review of the War

*(for the Coalition of African lesbians
hoping not to type-cast you; and not
to convict myself of political correctness)*

Yes, war is perhaps the main character here, lots of rape
and killing. Maiming, too. So take it off to the court
in the Hague. Somewhere in that torn countryside a man
and a boy come into view, damaged but destined to survive.
Their endurance against the odds – dead bodies
all around, a burnt-out bus for home, water &
food to be stumbled on out of sight – is a story
that buoys the reader battling waves of despair.

And for review, what might you ask, is missing?
The pre-war life of something vaguely known. Like a woman,
a bucket of water on her head, getting home unmolested.
Or a scene elsewhere of a parent taking the children (girls,
say, now in uniform, nudging modernity) to school.
In another frame a child is having a birthday party,
friends bringing presents. Missing . . . is something
of the thread of a slow pattern of living, disrupted.

In whose book do we fuss over the child's bedwetting,
because of war? Where do couples like us talk quietly
of a slippage in the partnership before it's too late:
nebulous things silenced in the clatter of bombs
and machetes? The pages needed to bring two people
into understanding that time and patience,
and care for the children might help them through
a wobbly patch, must be given over to rougher stuff.

So like a schoolboy with a dirty book to quote from, I mark
passages, to be restored, from the cut of censorship. Like here:
'Then, he will kiss her hand which is older than it was,
and love her for it; and be grateful for everything

they have gone through together. And those small duplicities
that await domestic grace, will be confessed
in that space, middle of nowhere, your web
of normalness keeping its shape.' End of quote.

Us, With a Slight Impediment

The mind is *sssh-ready*
Like a new-tuned instrument;
The matter is translated into mine
And yours for whom it was always meant.

These are the good old days
When song aspires to undo the war.
So we look at the lyrics between us
Each one built on a flaw.

Motherbirthdaypoem

I've been to Lisbon, if you want to know,
on that secret mission between ourselves.
And here I am on the 8.27
from Sheffield to London. World traveller, me.
Why am I thinking of your birthday now
that you live beyond the counting of days,
and turn up unawares like a conscience
we're relieved to admit was always there!

I'm on a train from Sheffield to London.
You must know Sheffield, you know everything.
I'm facing the wrong way, for what it's worth.
I sit in the quiet mobile-free coach,
something we'll talk about. Oh yes, I didn't
find that pastry-chef brother in Lisbon.

In Praise of the Community

The worst has happened here. And here,
thousands of miles apart. I'm watching
the survivors, some numb with anger,
others fraught with forgiveness. And
the few who join this voyeur's luxury
of rage cannot break free of the crowd's webbing.
I am baffled, suspicious, then ashamed.
But I'm alone in a room watching the television;
my restraints are in another country –
a woman and step-children, friends
who still think I'm the man I would like to be:
I imagine them, *out there*, miracle-working.
A reprieve for me, then, to be here alone.

So no hanging and . . . whatever is done
in your pulse of haste; no beatings,
no torture of an emotional kind.
I don't believe this, of course, but
how to account to people I know;
how to justify fifty years of reading
philosophy and writing poetry?
And beyond the people you know,
there is a community somewhere, wounded
in its own way, struggling to get by
without severed heads on the railings, perhaps
without the satisfaction of acts less showy.
I look at them, too, on television,
folk angry as I am, managing to restrain
the wayward by some thread so invisible –
it's an idea, a tradition, long-
established practice – that you fear
it won't hold. Most in this gathering
would have read less than I have, and not written

books: how can I admit that the learning
was in vain? So for now that's enough
to check me from further descent into self.

For C. J. Harris: Three Poems

In Memoriam, C.J. Harris 1910–2003

He taught us not to accept the boundaries
of the island: you could paint your *Gauguins*,
set down vast novels in its villages.
Those long-time heroes we kneel to – the kings
and prelates, the gods, the one Big Daddy –
are just fellas embarrassed by their fame
and the quality of their fans. That's why
they lurk in the rum-shop, ever hopeful.

Now he spoke to me of familiar things,
my long residence abroad, still no wife
this late in life; and concerns that seemed less
Antichrist than the unease of a mother.
And he said, face to the wall: how can you
pass on your estates, boy, without an heir?

Ladbroke Grove, '58

And we laughed at it, C. J. Harris' joke to us
on the jetty before sailing for the province,
that some habits over there would not be acceptable
to the Children of the House of Stapleton
abandoned now to the slow fate of ruin:
we must recall that even a great governor, back then
with his Latin, couldn't convince barbarians to the peace of Rome.
Ah, what sorts of questions will turn up now?

Tonight, Calgacus' speech to the Caledonians:
When I consider the motives we have for fighting . . .
I have a strong feeling that the united front you're showing
will mean the dawn of liberty for all of Britain.
And two boys whom we knew came by and said
the natives were getting restless at Notting Hill.

Homage to an Old Master

'The King of France had none of his own teeth.
And still he had a wife. And ruled the country.'
That was our introduction to Louis XIV
by C. J. Harris who by then had gaps in his mouth.
Apparently the King was only forty at the time,
which seemed a great age, of course, maybe CJ's age;
and CJ, too, had a wife but no country to rule:
so do we pity the king of France, or what?

Some boys said in those days you could replace
your own teeth with those of a poor man
caught in the street, or you could have teeth made
from a hard wood, like greenheart, sewn into
your mouth and painted, so who's to know they weren't
your own except the wife when she kissed you;
for she would have to be careful of splinters.
And we pitied the mouth of the Queen of France.

But little did we know: CJ was too artful
to say that the King had not only a wife
but *mistresses*, who must have known about the teeth.
Though when you inherited a country
and then fought all those *wars*, and signed peace *treaties*
and lived in places like Versailles, and spoke French
like a native, maybe not having your teeth
at the age of forty was no big deal.

So I open wide for the dentist, a man
who goes skiing abroad at my expense
(Oh snow! Ah, rich, young things!). He assures me
that my restored mouth is better than greenheart
with enamel from felled, wild elephant (think of
the digestion, the smile at bedtime to *Madame
Fastidious*): now like a veritable swissbank of loot
I can pretend to be nothing special.

To My Mother, the Art Critic

I put it down, I say, to my mother, my first art critic.
Back then, oh, in another country, a woman in her prime
nicely contained in that dress we know, its modesty protesting
those *The Lady at her Piano* snaps for the album. But that was
    Before –
yes, we've had too many images of After –
that was when, on a Sunday afternoon after church,
Anancyman came to the house and arranged a sitting:
In the drawing-room a detail of her dress is out of place.

II

No, of course, you do not understand. I come back to this scene
decades later on a day in Sheffield laid out to be painted.
I pause in mid-stride, the rinsed landscape too clean for February;
the bruised sky of yesterday clearing up, a scent of elsewhere drifting
indoors, from the garden. I think of men in berets and cravats
at the *salon* – of a provincial Degas whose aim was to trap you
    dancing.
Or an island Renoir with no fear and hatred of women.
Of your afterlife drawing suitors to worship at Orsay and
    Marmottan.

III

So, yes, I'm thinking back to the small accident in the churchyard
(sermons do not prepare you for the dangers of uneven ground);
and then to your pampered ankle after lunch, caught on canvas,
along with the vicar and headmaster providing the conversation.
The boy with the made-up name was praised for the likeness
of the bandage on the lady's foot: he could have been a medic as well
as artist. Not bad, you said, the sternest judge. And then you asked:
But how are you going to paint my other shoe, over it?

A Little Puzzle

Enter an African with a fish on his head:
Now how do you account for that? my friend.
If he's near the sea or the lake he'd know
that's not the way to do it. On the other hand
he may have sold the basket or calabash
on the long trek inland, carrying the fish
as evidence of an expedition gone wrong.

He may have been using the fish as a hat,
not having an umbrella. Or as a symbol
to show the world that living in a climate
this harsh mocks all ambition.
So give to the needy, cancel Africa's debt
and think better of yourself for suppressing
a thought of Africa turning up on the doorstep.

And in comes the smartarse, Mr know-it-all.
Imagine, he says, this man out of Africa,
still with the fish on his head. He's near here
on the corner of a busy street, with the markets
laid out, stalls heavy with fruit of land and sea;
and yet he draws a little crowd to view
the fish on his head. In his hands, dumb-bells

at the ready, he stands erect, a little tank
of water on his head, the fish swimming
in its private sea. He juggles and jokes,
he entertains mothers and their children,
full of shopping, with tales they'd like to believe:
he encourages them to laugh at him
now that they can't make jokes about religion.

The Widow's Eulogy

Well then, there were two things that alerted you to the tone
of the marriage, the fact that the new widow gave the Eulogy –
strange in itself – and that she canvassed opinion about the husband:
he was known, of course, to be a superb cook
a traveller and – dare one say it here? – a favourite with the ladies.
It's useful to think that the compiling of notes on someone
so recently close to you is another of those activities
intended to contain the grief. Anyway, she seems OK.

She inhabits the podium as if a preacher born to it.
The dress is, ah, fetching as is a US Secretary of State's.
She surveys the congregation, severe and businesslike
in her glasses, and begins the tribute. Much of what she says
we might have said, though *his* generosity goes wider than we knew.
And yes, the love of cooking, the sociability is stressed.
Before the pause, before the punch-line: And then she says:
We never suffered food-poisoning. He never gave me AIDS.

Scarves and Benches

Scarves and benches come together only at those times
when the mind taking a rest without your noticing
is jolted out of it and cautions you to pay heed.
That's why on losing my scarf I think of Horace, a mad fellow
to those who didn't know him: for what do you say of a man
without means erecting monuments to a relative
who thought him mad? First, there was a bench on the island,
then other benches in places where the sitters would be foreign.

Scarves and benches come together now that I've left another
valued strip of silk on some bus or pavement indifferent
to the vanity that once sought it out and thought its splash of
    colour
a small trick to put upon a grown-up day. I liked the benches
for their wooden life, random and not designed to be immortal.
Not sky-threatening, close to the ground as if in tune
with a man from a small island, or of small stature, a man
in casual mourning for a world that, surely, no one made.

I deny that this shedding of silk at random will serve to link
one journey with another in any special way. Though it hurts a
    little
to be anonymous once again; and the chance collector,
proud of this find that won't defend its shape as if it mattered,
is your invention. So scarves and benches come together as when
your sentence not written down won't be recalled, and shufflings
of the grammar all refuse to fit. So what can I say? Scarves
are less permanent than benches. Scarves are a good form of litter.

Cracks

Then one morning you're tying your shoelaces
and there they are, two more-than-cracks in your favourite shoe
which couldn't have been there the day before; or are you past
observing details so close to home? And, yes,
for leather suddenly to give out without warning is unsettling
(though, on reflection, this is how things happen; for how terrifying
to base your philosophy on anticipating surprise and accident!)
Nevertheless the unease will not confine itself to shoes.

So of course you go back to the bathroom mirror
(remembering the betrayal in that hotel room
when an unaccustomed arrangement of glass caught you unawares,
showed you shapes your vanity never knew):
you go back to the mirror and test your courage
on a safe bit of self. Not quite as before but it knows – surely,
something: the god of biology knows – this can't be replaced
as easily as shoes. So what to do? You vow to take more care of
        the shoes.

From *A Family Epic*: Ten Poems

1 Ceremony at Maracuene, Mozambique

The animal pound and flower bed
back home
were round. The bronzed cistern

breeding froglife
at the back of the house
seemed the right shape.

From boxing ring and track
to call-it-stadium
we all worship in the round.

And what new marvel
(Mr. Marco Polo & Columbus)
you bringing back now

from your travels? –
For already it have calabash and Zulu-
hut safe in the museum.

Nothing, man, nothing
but a chance meeting under a tree
in a place I can't remember.

No jump-up and foolishness;
all low-key and calm:
Man, woman dress-up for they thing.

'Nuf to say it shape like
something ancient. Quiet quiet.
No applause. Sky-henge. Magic.

2 God of the Flat

You go back to those days when the debate
made less sense, when you were privileged
to live in a large house, and one duty,
they said, to out-think the undeserving,
was to construct a god big as the house.
And we tried over the years for a twelve-
roomed god, clever enough to stand all night
at the front and back yards and on those bits

of land worked by folk whose gods were too small
to travel. Fruit-trees in the garden, pigs
and chickens had their gods. Then we were safe,
till the logic hit us that friends who lived
in more-roomed houses would despise the size
of our god; and we fled the scene in shame.

3 A Verandah Ceremony

This is where the kitten died
This is where the kitten died
In the yard below, unfenced
The wild dogs came as if on horses,
Or a Lord's Resistance Army
With machetes, with spears and rifles
The wild dogs came all claws and barking.
This is where the kitten died.

This new *new* kitten three weeks old
Must avoid a kitten's fate
Must clear the house of lizards
Bugs and insects and not stray
Beyond the safety gate where the dogs
All tooth and claw still lie in wait

Where the dogs still lie in wait.

4 Apologie

How dare you, fool
To offer that sound
And think to say

This thing that thing
That maybe only humans
Feel the need

To be glad or sad
About? And that's the easy
Test of matching

Word and thing: pride
Drives you on
To glimmer . . . tremor

To nearly . . . maybe
To . . . is it? Is there? Listen!
All so quiet, lost & . . .

(This Ur time before
One thing and another
Till *yes*, nebulous pulse

In the soup
That leads to, ah –
Light. Sound. Song. Your face.

5   An Act in the Comedy

The eye gives out
in the middle of my book
as if to deny a destiny

for reading and writing.
So the joke stops
at this new insult

to dignity. The way back
from the dentist
through the College park

is risky in the holiday season.
A heart-attack here
(not anywhere, but not here)

where no one might come
in time, isn't funny;
can't be made witty.

But steer clear of
the path more taken
where some passing reveller

in the spirit of the occasion
might pause and look around
and take charge

and put the boot in
and put the boot in
to initiate this

no eye, no book
no book, no teeth
ceremony.

6   As Spoken by a Great Aunt to a Niece Whose Name is Lost

They went after the big picture,
the boys who could see big sky
above hurdles in the way;
and how much like high-jumpers
they trained and trained. Oh,
the frenzy and passion of it all.
But some were not natural athletes
and settled for moving
one foot in front of another.
As you know that's the wrong way
to go in a race where luck
sets you down behind folk

heading for glory. We didn't have
the legs for it, and settled
for a life behind the victory line
and (we have our pride) called it home.
Family who set their sights higher,
and collect the trophies
and still use our name,
and promise to defend us,
look down when they can
and talk of the old days: at least
you don't have vertigo, they say.

7 Progress

After the stroke she aims to walk again,
out of the room, down the stairs, like herself.

She can't be protected from harm as if
the park is a huge mound, slippery with mud.

Old-time care, yes, and a will they didn't know
she had, led one step to shame the other.

So now for the park, green as before with
strollers to mock her – a man and his dog;

and *she* limp-scaling the ground with her days-
old bread, good for the hand; good for the ducks.

8   Family Matters

So don't talk to *her* about dreams, as if
they're things you encourage: she is fifty now
and he is eighty. So who's to control
the old stories, now that it's three against one:
daughter, her partner, and a loss still fresh.
Theirs is the higher ground, he will slip towards
age and bafflement. Then he remembers
that he is old and baffled. Enough said.

That he had threatened to send her to school
in a far place where no one spoke English;
and that he counted her fingers and toes
and came up with a new number each time;
and that he wrote to the starving of the world
to rouse them to what she left on her plate,
he pleads guilty to. And here she is now,
all intact, partnered; and speaking English.

9   For the Unknown Member

Of the family? Why not: you needn't go back
into pre-history which, as some wits say
takes you all the way to the generation before last.
So she's out there somewhere, man-handled
into the family story, unaware
that x centuries down the line someone
who doesn't know her as an ancestor, is prickled
into a fantasy that she might exist.

Of your name I won't speculate:
that would be to lose you to something *generic*
part of a tribe already known. For your fear
in producing someone who in time produced me
I offer in contrition a doctor in the family,
to assist birth. To honour you I will dress
like a stranger, and wail and chant till this
is not about me. Then I'll share you with others.

10   Little Miracles

These are the people you know, there's no point
wishing others in their place to prod you
into that challenge likely to excite
the biographer. These ordinary-
seeming folk, generous and punitive
in turns, heroic in understated
unexpected ways are perhaps the best
that might have happened to you. So praise them.

Praise the mother for not doing away
with you, as she might, suspecting the worst.
Praise the smaller accidents in a life
that didn't quite happen. Praise the comic turn
from the pulpit who baffled the audience
with the startling gift of loaves and fishes,
and endless living. Praise now the goddess
of jokes and foolishness, busy elsewhere.

Woman on the Verandah, Reading

At the book-signing he spells out a name
and the novelist, practised at this art
writes a tribute to someone's sister
managing for a moment to set her image fluttering
into interest. The woman, a good reader,
lived in this country and worked in its hospitals
and is back now to reclaim her island
of high-swaying palms and fresh colour.
He can imagine in this new recruit to his prose
someone who takes to the waves most days
and comes home lively as seawater.

And the brother recalls her on the verandah
of a new house. Inside is a painting on the wall
to make them uneasy; men linked together by a rope
round the neck, hands tied at the wrist; a country at war.
Replaying the joke against herself, the nurse
imagines these captives washed and dressed,
one tending the family, another doing something
not worth noting; then, perhaps much older
coming to rest where she used to work.

These men will not let her go. She sits there
still with the page unturned, her mind uninvaded
by the richness of prose that well-describes her.
Who knows if she's conscious of the restless sea,
of chunks of her life that didn't travel, of a big book
sent in lieu of a visit? There's a lizard on the wall,
the cat wandering off; and a boy with a cutlass
in her sights, toying with the tall grass next-door.
There she sits, book in hand, like a portrait.

Woman on the Verandah, Reflects

And if, indeed, he had lost his life
in some foolish, heroic cause
like converting Africans to his god
as if he, a converted African
were not warning enough
against what some call parody,
cutting his cloth to his cloth,
making each day seem like the Sabbath
and us in need of salvation:
this not-quite prodigy framed
with brothers of another colour
in the group photograph
granting, mocking ordinariness –
as if, indeed, he could be saved
as bric-à-brac from that life
and transported back to this life –
a clean white house with a view,
trees in the garden tight-fisted
with fruit called forth too soon.

Men and boys, heroes all,
like cousin Reggie who bolted
the yard at fifteen and ended up
a soldier in lands we learnt to spell
in places on a map where others live;
he was not the one at relief
of the port of Antwerp in '44;
that story is for another time.

But these thoughts slide off
the lines of the new house,
set down lighter on its hill-top
than its predecessors
in the lease-hold inner-cities.

Or further back to the Old Place
of stubborn family lore
heavy with generations
of expectation, of journeyings
ever outwards. Now a brother
blows in from the world to report
to her like a son, like a grandson
of marvels she must credit.

He'll be pleased with himself:
there's no reason why
he shouldn't be pleased with himself:
He will risk his heart
against the ocean. She must prepare
healthy meals and remember
not to be tired or ill.

So, will they sit for the portrait, this time?
and deny it's for a record
too carelessly dealt with.
After so much disturbance and movement
a period of calm on the wide verandah
is what the doctor orders;
and some island Rembrandt
with a weakness for rum and history
as well as paint in his eye
will pretend to glimpse beyond the present
to the slim girl in school uniform
on her ladies-frame bicycle;
or else toying with being adult
in the afternoon haze, with a parasol.
Inside, the music without words
will be decoded for politics.
And the visitor, decades
of world-knowing on his face will confess
'I'll give the pyramids a miss
because of the vertigo,' – will confess

to have failed at things she never tried.
It will be a time of nothing and everything.
He will agree that Ethiopia
has been a long time Christian
and answer that worrying question about St. Augustine.
He will report, like John Simpson, from Baghdad.

At the Redland Hotel, Stamford Hill

The basement room lets in the light
and breeze through the grille of the open window.
As the TV doesn't work I lie in bed
reading Lowell's *Life Studies*
killing an hour or so in contrition
before the necessary telephone call of the morning.

This might be punishment enough: to wake
in a low time, loo and shower shared
along the corridor, family pride honoured
only in the clean sheets (the Australian patron
true to her word that nothing would crawl
and scuttle here during the night).
And somehow Lowell's absurd and beguiling
family seem OK in this light.

Yesterday, not knowing the future
I was thinking how to write up
that old scene at the Paddington Baths
in – was it – '57? with Sunday morning orators
and their congregation of the unwashed,
staged for my education.

Those amateur Ciceros, less of *The Murder Trials*,
more of the *Letters to Friends* brought
Grenadian and Tobagian accents
to the poor Roman theatre of bath-time –
urging Khrushchev & Co. to do the black man
a favour, and go to war.

Despite everything I think of myself without irony
as a man of property, lucky in my world.
So I wake in a basement on the Seven Sisters Road.
(Who were those sisters? Lowell's
would be dream institutions housing
our brightest lesbian daughters;
though if we're talking families, then a grandmother,
a mother from Montserrat would not lack
the colour of these New Englanders.)

And I, too, remember taking a body home
to be buried, though I doubt, whether like Lowell's
mother, she travelled First Class in her DC10.
These thoughts, stirring my weakness
to be blown off-track, will swirl into something
like resentment, unless I call home now.

2

Heading for the phone I try not to think
of the other man's nine month's daughter
signalling him, with a dab of water on her cheek,
to shave. *I will be at fault. I am at fault.*
I mean it. The phone-box broken, I think
of options in life, like owning America,
and wonder if that, too, will drive you mad.
Like Commander Lowell, my new twin,
I have a mock title and am growing irrelevant;
and must tread that line (I'm sober, mother, lover)

between dignity and ridicule.
Lowell's nostalgic last afternoon with Uncle
Devereux Winslow was when he was five.
I am sixty-three: how far is that now, from five?

So What's It Like?

Ah, some days it's like being in the right place
where the light though good for painting
doesn't expose you to the glare of disapproval
of passers-by colouring in their canvases in advance.
Though, happily, there's enough distraction in the world,
real blood and circuses, or in the private killer under the skin
to divert this people's creative energy from its logic.

And then there are days when a picture, though dismissed
as art, holds its appeal. Like the late-night movie,
the thriller where the OK guy, nice wife & family
attracts attention of the Evil One
who satans his way past Our Hero's (why me?) defences.

Ah, but relief will come in time, good detective and all that.
The family, in the end, will be stronger than before,
the world put to rights. That is your cue to say:
This is only a movie, look what's happening out there!
And, yes, anyway; some days here it's not so bad.

The Search

They saw him coming, of course, talked to him
in a language meant for grown-ups: structurally,
the house is sound, load-bearing walls intact;
a bit of damp, y'know, in the basement, underground
river, and all that; and the street, though tricky to say
like that Cambridge College, is something you'll soon
be using to advantage. The gentrification
has begun, the old dying or being moved out, couples
and restaurants taking their place. And, hey presto,
the search is done. Oh yes. Legally OK.

And on his private list of things to check
nothing is ticked off: how to read the statistics
of where it's safe to live? For in this street,
in this town, if what they say is right,
someone is pretending to be something else;
and three, maybe four, ah, torturers of a domestic kind
still smirk in their sitting-rooms; and who will point out
the house where a dirty word we needn't say squats
and soils our politics? Again, between here
and the High Street how is the resident murderer
without a scar on his face, to be identified?

When he invites a friend to toast this latest Safe House
she says well done, darling, and wonders
if he's earned it, for even though his hands
are clean she thinks perhaps he's lucky with
neighbours from hell who won't invade his sleep
as they do hers. Sensing her resentment
he tells a story from the poet Che Qianzi,
of two people dreaming of an elephant,
and whether they dreamt the same elephant –
for an elephant is very large to manage when you're asleep.
And she relents and wishes him luck.

But what can he do to complete this search
and cleanse the street? The Agency, uninterested
in this level of hygiene, does not supply
new air, or a soap that launders memory.
So he must compromise, like staying in an old marriage
till it becomes less bad. Or because it's the same
or worse elsewhere. (For outside the house
the world comes to us in a blitz of Headlines
and friends fly away from don't-call-them massacres.)
So, dear god, pretend that life is long and you are old;
and settle for a scaled-down Truth and Reconciliation
Commission for your street. And like the parent
body over there, don't ask for reparations.

I'm Hiding

(She speaks)

Yes, it worked those times when
we were maybe three and five
and always wanted to discover

the one hiding in the next room
or under the table, no embarrassment
at squeals of delight

on discovery. It was the best
game ever, even after the squealing
tightened into something else,

and the seekers were no longer
family. Times remembered
when I laid a trail so private

only you could find me:
how clever you were tracing
clues softer than thrown ribbon

or rose-petals, clues
sometimes soft as scent dissolving
into air. When you began to lose

your way I had to mark the ground
with harder evidence – things
branded valuable in themselves –

to my hiding-place. A mistake
as I emerged this time,
that time and found the markers gone.

Oh, my darling, I have hidden
long in alien places
guarding treasure for someone

loyal to the game. But they say
you are bored with such memory,
that you, too, have grown up.

The Fruit, the Tree

And what do you say to the child
To calm her and stop the tears:
She can't understand why the fruit

She'd watched grow to perfection
Is now in a bowl inside.
The thought to separate fruit

From tree seemed a good idea
Before putting it back
Where it belonged. Why can't you

Who must know everything
Put these things right? No one told her
It had to be like this.

Explanations are hateful; everything
Is hateful: she won't believe it.
And must the tree die?

Years later you agree:
No use hanging on to things
That flatter you. The man

With the blade is your friend,
The best pruner in town.
So let's pretend you're the tree

Ripe where you don't need to be.
This fruit cannot be good
For you. Trust me. Trust me.

Town & Country Protest

(remembering Gavin Ewart)

It must be the one where Kenneth Williams
plays the doctor, with his stethoscope,
and the joke is he's a horse-doctor with a big instrument;
and he says: Can you get down on all fours, Madame?
And she says: Why, good doctor; like this?
And he says: *Now* I know where things are.

Again she must make those noises that embarrass her
off the farm. And what are you doing now, good doctor?
He says: Seeing how many hands you measure
here and here. And that's not a hand, dear doctor:
that feels like a rude party of country lovers
thud thudding through my right of way.

Dreaming, Waking

In your dreams your body is in worse shape
than when you wake to the attritions of the day:
how often must you fall off those high buildings,
or be on the run for murdering this or that unlikely rival?
The light chases all those daemons away,
and there's no priest hovering over breakfast
with the rites. Even the troublesome toenail
turning to soil and plant-life, is less scary after the bath.

So, a working world of trivia and distant killing
is not the worst that can happen; small betrayals
of partners and friends embarrass you
but keep the species busy in ways that snakes, say,
and cattle would find difficult. Yes, to wake to outwit
the hitman and the Aidsgod makes you frisky.

A Politically-Correct Marriage

Romance it was with that leap of imagination in Sheffield
when her wave at the station added warmth to the day
that so far had been brightened only by snow; and he,
a man so robbed in confidence, hesitated before waving back;
so she greeted her friend instead, a woman wholesome as the fresh
        snow.
But here's a problem for a girl so caring, confusing a sad man in
        public:
don't be embarrassed, her quick smile said, don't be embarrassed
her bashful eyes said, as she rehearses the embrace with her friend.

Back then, the story had no shape; before the children came
    along,
so that now no one thinks of one partner without the other;
though, it must be said, there's sometimes pause for reflection,
    lacking in,
y'know, *Horse & Hound*. Or *Fox & Firkin*. Like checking the
    Solicitor's
between the butcher and the cake-shop. So they come in handy,
this couple, when we give up on other *items* that depress us;
on the rich north & poor south, on biblical fish & the ocean.
Palestine & Israel. Archbishop & Actress. Poet & poem.

Election Evening in France

There's no point in denying that you live in France,
so don't bring me Segolene and Sarko gossip
as if fresh-minted in Texas, or Abidjan.
It's true of course that Segolene dresses too well
to be President and might have to settle for
being a Frenchwoman who got the politics wrong.
And your sparky Sarko, sprung from his low level
of gravity, stands tall. Tall as the tallest Gaul!

So here we are on the night in question, distanced
from *Concorde* and *Bastille*. The temper of this house
will be maintained whoever wins. We who can't vote,
are gathered for dinner and learned comment
in the spirit of our hosts. Subjects for debate
between courses will be: La Rochefoucauld: is he
still witty? And how sound is the numerate Pascal?
La Fayette: is *The Princess of Cleves* a novel?

At the Court of Felix Anadobi

The old French President claims that the English
would not find us on the map, a little joke
of Tulle's, he was always good for a laugh,
we shall miss him. But the new boy talks the talk
of his office; and says the troopers will stay
and defend us: *the honour of France*. Good
to have friends who won't cut and run the moment
things get rough for their boys and girls overseas.

So we're here in sunny Anodobiland
getting on with our job of creating
a culture you only dream about: no child-
soldiers, no foolishness about religion
to put us on the newsreels. No oil or diamonds.
Here, the children of the ruler are trained
to write verses and record songs critical
of the parent. They're graded as *literature*.

Elsewhere, the people philosophise. My son
is unofficial Leader of the Opposition
and not in gaol. My younger daughter, a fine shot,
will assassinate me cleanly when I get bored
with things, and will be a heroine of sorts.
To avoid bloodshed Tulle's men will stay on
and decide which child will rule, sparing the people
violence and disruption of their studies.

59 or 60%?

You're right, of course: in the end are planes going to crash
or Empires crumble if this average student falls
on this or that side of the line? And yet it matters
for your view of self, respect for the subject and all that;
for the institution, even, to get this right – part of the fantasy
that at some other time, back then, guidance had been firm:
call it a parallel Christ, a community of the selfless,
a home-grown Socrates urging us back from convenience.

Nonsense, you say, as we pause to think of the wide-boy
blagging his way into power; of the near-doctor who skipped
     classes
and passed the exam, and of our friend who thought of a short-cut
towards flying the plane. These are the things we're smug about.
The concern is nearer home: right or wrong answers
may not tell you much; but the way of getting there must be graded.
And what of the gap between *here* and *there*? So I ask again:
does this one edge above the line where your planes won't crash?

Hand & Eye

This is the burning-pot, last time the rice;
tonight, it's the specially bought organic potatoes.
So, time to sit back and ponder why it's gone wrong.
You never were a ball-player, a Sobers, a Beckham.
Even juggling with Latin embarrassed you with its spillage
of meaning. So why persist in thinking, after a life's experience,
you could better what the Americans said of one of their presidents,
and try to chew gum and scratch your arse at the same time.

To cook the meal and write the poem is the issue:
when will you give up this fantasy? You recall the young
Shirley Temple at the piano announcing to the audience
that she would play and sing *at the same time.*
And you think, all these years after Temple; all these men
in the world maintaining two families *at the same time*;
the politicians conducting war and peace *at the same time*:
is it too much to ask yourself to do these two things at once?

Interdenominational

Seats like pews; and you notice that folk here
don't seem too stricken by self-consciousness
to be credible: nurse comes out and calls
a name, and you half expect Lilly Cross
to be in the wrong place, and flutter by,
a flower on a stem, against the cheek;
to play the 'I-can-still-sound-like-a-girl'
voice of the courtesan on *Songs of Praise.*

And not bothering with flowers, Lilly
answers and is wheeled in, cheerful enough.
As the god of satire and the god
of Biology struggle for the laughs
you become a convert of this priesthood
patching up bits of life yet to be lived:
here's a restful one back from confession
heading for an exit which no one blocks.

A Trial

She was represented by the best Legal mind
that they knew, though he couldn't make the trial;
yet, the witnesses had known her all their life.
Out of respect the trial would take place
in the comfort of her home; the male court-
scene would give way to something less intimidating:
a table set for dinner, and the family
acting as if this was not being viewed by strangers.

The son would be the Judge. He deepened his voice
and enunciated as if this was something he had trained for.
The charge in question had the force of a four-letter word
in the singular. The husband-prosecutor
tried to speak from both sides of his mouth. The daughter,
standing in for the defence, was magnificent
and nearly convinced all present that the accused,
though lacking appetite, had been known to tell a joke.

A Story for Today

At that point lots of things died; the world went dark and dark
    wasn't a metaphor.
And no one knew if anything of note had happened. Except that
    footsteps moving away
From the scene paused, to return now with the unsure tread of the
    curious;
And then the laying on of hands as if to trick hurt into healing, as a
    name difficult to pronounce
Seemed as good as yours. And here's a place to end the story. Except
    that someone who might be listening
Would want a better ending. 'Crime up, the quality of life down',
    can't be the quote to go out on.
So let's concentrate on reading between the lines: imagine something
    new is being said
About life not death. About becoming the worst. About
    understanding that this might not be the worst.

And so, in this first line of the second part of the story, the speaker
    is restored to energy:
This is a second chance, the revival, restoration of something like
    sight, things magicked back
From oblivion, like the fitting of that first pair of glasses – Yes, here
    comes the imagery –
The lost wife caught sight of on the 31 bus in Kilburn, oh, Merry
    Christmas, 1963: she was not,
My Lord, one with gold bracelet on her ankle, or tattoo on the
    shoulder. As always
The frame of this picture is adjustable. For look at these two nuns in
    the park, a joke rippling their habits,
Sharing the canvas with browning bodies on the Côtes d'Azur and
    pallid ones in Urology in a Sheffield waiting room –
All this – and maybe more – restored to you in a story to be
    continued.

Poem

Then someone looks up from her book to see an elephant in
    the garden.
That's what you need to restore the magic and mystery of
    literature
in these days of hardship. The poets of small titles are
    unnourishable, as we say,
as they allow no distraction or diversion to colour the verse:
things that get in the way of a slim idea's logic – too suggestive
of messiness in a life, or of a hinterland of experience too large
    for our time –
must be *genred* out. So frame after frame will be reduced in a game
where the detail is all, a bland pattern of syllables left to be
    admired.

So now we have it, a poem fit for today, the subject more or less
    solitary,
pondering the crossword of a life; being understated and stoic
about mishaps at the paths long taken; eschewing the vulgarity
    of old time
hero and anti-hero – oh, don't go there – for the more wearable
    badge
of victim: a shrewd assessment of the scribbler's small talent and
    rewards.
In this unenvied life I'm trying to smuggle the dream of earlier
    years,
of better titles, *The Princess of Cleves*, *The Old Curiosity Shop*,
and a place in your tight pentameter for a malignant dwarf called
    Daniel Quilp.

Apologies for disturbing the neat arrangement of words to admire,
words perhaps to console the sick, but sculptured like the
    shrinking self,
making the healthy and the living, suspect blackmail: no one
    inside your poem

works through the backache, or has an adventure for the hell of it,
　　or goes
to the loo. That's why I'm going to buck the trend and call this
　　moment
not *A Princess of Cleves* or *An Old Curiosity Shop*, not even *A Bible*
or *A Koran*. But, thinking of that woman stirred by the elephant in
　　her garden,
I'm going to call this arrangement of words, *Gulliver's Travels, II*.

Back Stories

1

He's got an illness they can joke about
at work: if he chose a chocolate biscuit
or a sweet from the tin, would he pass out
right here on the floor and need mouth to mouth?
The thought both giggly and alarming
plunges the office into fringe theatre.
We're all responsible folk here, *of course*,
so no sweet thing for you today, my lad.

2

And is the same thing that kill that fella
who come home after years in Canada,
and did up that planter's place on the road
to the airport. You'd think a man like that
would have stayed abroad where it had treatment
for his problem. Instead, to come and build
mausoleum for yourself, is a thing
that don't make any sense to me, at all.

A Few Lines from Philoctete's Epic

(After Omeros *– on Walcott's 73rd)*

I

Eh eh, so wonders never cease, boy, never mind
that the second coming going be a man with a grudge
come to tief what all you left behind last time:

remember the last preacherman come here to mug
the faithful with prayer for we sin of hurricane
and volcano? Now I'm not the one to judge

how this work out. I don't live here. But all the same
since we couldn't have Horace, still mad in Antigua
with 'Elvis Lives', or C.J. Harris to explain

how the church get trashed to spite the Believer,
they give we instead a character from a book
with name we can't pronounce even if we sober.

He come limping through the ash as if he have foot,
though they say he cure. Like he setting up to claim
miracle when he go walk straight again. The book

don't say so but I know what I know. And then again ?
maybe we lucky to have this well-known figure
from Gros Ilet and Ma Kilman rumshop come

to convert the village to literature. Better a
man-sized wound for weapon than chigger in you toe
to rouse up the people to claim their metaphor.

After the baptism in the bush we must know
that obeah works: what with the bubbling basin
and woman baying at she ancestors – Philo

shin stop smell and bite. That's a fact. It is written.
Though he sometimes still change the dressing in he mind,
that's just human. Call him sorefoot; it's your history.

II

Philoctete, whose brain proved weaker than his mate,
Achille's whose antennae could pick up old Africa,
tuned in, like a swiftless uncle, to a local place
trashed by hurricane, cleansed by volcano. (If you can't
walk under the sea, even in dream, in case you drown
you have to be sensible.) And Africa,

he says, is any place we wake up far from home
after a life of misery. Washed up here on sand
hot enough to addle brains, he bet that Crusoe

without a woman, did bawl to heaven for Helen –
that mirage in a lemon dress – as reparation
for what in past life used to sniff and growl at him.

                    *

So he is sitting there half-way up Miss Dove's
backdoor step just where Mr Frederick used to sit
waiting for his dinner – a house that passed already

into history. (Ruins, boy, *ruins*.) Now the risk
of telling one old man from the next, is to hear
his story. You know that you can't afford to miss

this opening, for on small island, memory
is your hinterland, and Epic is we middle name.
So this is like a parenthesis before we

take our bearings again, somewhere where we can claim
an abandoned villa in the safe zone. Phil will
talk about sea-battles, and peacemaking between

the young rascals over you know who, with Achille
and Hector playing the arse, when everything end
in tragedy: Hector dead in the boat he sail

too fast on land; Achille coming through in the end.
And the widow, looking nice, y'know!. Miss Helen
send a chill, again, to coldcircuit the system

End of detour. But maybe they don't tell lie when
they say that publican and sinner sound the same;
because no one wants to hear Philoctete crying

foul over losing out to the pig-breeder's prime
bits of text, all that guilt stalking Helen in her
no-trespassing dress. Where's the lyric to the shine

Philo take to the Irishwoman lost out here;
the times he hears her embroidered birds loud and clear,
no smouldering coalpit of a Plunket in the air.

     III

Asleep on the island, his eyes open. A game
the blind don't play, not even a wily Seven Seas
with eye everywhere. Now with rod and mitre again

he chac-chacing into town, leaping like the breeze
when Boxing Day come round; three musicians, drummer,
the warriors and Achille marching on Castries.

But wait, he hallucinating; must be hunger
though he still not hungry: Unless he get poorly
not eating nothing so far. Maybe he done dead

already and gone to Art or verse – some holy
book parabling his life! So why does this Polish
waitress up in Canada, her lipstick come-on

red as a wound still prickle and keep him feverish?
And he remember, too, the ritual with Ma Kilman,
like a woman, licking the sweat off his face

with a rag, ice on the tongue, her body swaying
with the improving work. If he truly released
from the sore, he must sail with his mind surveying

from a distance things that he never used to see;
like imagining bits of the Book where your life
don't figure, appreciating new company

like the white-haired woman, neither mother nor wife
you neglect, though she shame you still; not for the foot
but for not knowing your history: the *Sioux*, in life,

was not a B film that break down and cause riot
at the *Rialto* matinée; the Dakotas
likewise, more than a couple of mid-western hick

states you didn't settle in. Thanks for the Dakotas
Miss Catherine Weldon (Well done.) Now, we's family.
Travelling not so hard, then. Philo crossing borders

like his friend Achille walking back to Africa
under the sea. The critics who can't swim can pause
here for company. Check out the foot. Have a chat.

A Bad Time

It's a bad time, your book
Is no consolation. Past midnight
And your present partner has not
Been identified. It's raining
On the tramps in the street.
Past midnight, time for the medicine.

And when the book fails to satisfy
Give praise to the mind's rebellion.
For the partner, there's still
A hundred and ninety-five countries
In the world. For you and the tramps
It will be morning. Soon.

2

from Human Rites

West Indian Myth 1

In the beginning was Man
standing still, Man in a hurry

hunting new skins in London
like Man beginning late.

In the beginning was evening,
White Studies on the State trapping

Man, breast-feeding, thigh-
beating him into mess, submission – his body

blackening with the victory scars.
In the beginning Man wrapped his past

in Community Relations like a left-
over bandage to entertain his friends;

and after all the fun, he ended up
years later, right where he began.

West Indian Myth 3

I am not a mugger, madam,
as you can see by my dress and

(excuse me, you won't be needing these
any more) manners. Note that my teeth

are all my own freshly brushed
and not blackened by obscene language.

Let me kiss you as the lover of your
choice (I am not, you see, prejudiced,

though a male chauvinist by persuasion
and clumsy with animals). One more thing:

I have misplaced my identity
with my card and must give you this

(forgive me) and this and this to know me by
when vengeance comes, when you are hysterical.

West Indian Myth 4

Third-generation poem recording
the trip, skirmishes, decades

of neglect. Mutation and revision
still accord it a link

with prehistory.
Prehistory is a joke in a library book

granting the status of fossil
to a newly-composed text, heavy

with apology, with deaths
to make itself seem real.

West Indian Myth 5

A grandson distances, reconnects
the house to torn memory.

You will drift back, near-parasite,
to this now strategic outpost.

Here, where once was city,
raw waves break upon the shore: gulls,

ships, whiff of long-
abandoned family force obedience

out of you, out of all. Fact
will not dissolve into Myth

as you plead old age, incompetence.
For dying will be harder.

West Indian Myth 6

And tourists came to the hot island
to smell native armpits, to screw

in the fields, while god sent
foreign storms and earthquakes

to puritanize the Myth. So the drought
that followed was well done.

Now holiday-island exiles slum it
in the cities of their dreams, sniffing

at old armpits, ready for the thug
of hurricane, of earthquake

disguised as the natives.

The Boy of the House

The ruin of the house, he lies on his stomach, womanless.
The boy is in water, frog-like, his mouth tastes of sea-weed.
He is looking at the rose-garden, it's not there
No longer at the front of the house –
Of what used to be the house . . .

The rose-garden is now at the bottom of the sea
And the boy throws a line, then another
To prevent more of the house drifting away.
He does this instead of growing into middle-age, or going abroad:
The boy is a great source of worry.

The Man Who Stayed at Home

He sits at home looking at the mountains.
He hears a young girl practising her scales.
Snap, say the tourists
taking him back to Boston, to Hamburg

to colour the winter. Sagging, on his verandah, the man
is all that's left of this once-great house
where no one learned to play the piano –
Chekhov of the tropics, say the tourists.

He waits for heirs
to return from the North with plunder and confidence
to rebuild, their link with this place unbroken:
will they use heads or hands for this?

The man watches and dreams of reunion
with the concert pianist reclaiming her instrument,
as familiar mountains edge closer
thinking him last of his line.

Seconds

Though they called themselves SECOND THOUGHTS
they knew what they were. They were seconds.

Raymond was the second son, Franco was pipped
at the post in the 800 yards that mattered

and Max just failed to win the Island Scholarship.
From runner-up to hand-me-down is a fate

few escape, so the lads decided to *organize*
a future. It grew to fill up the middle part

of their lives, like long walks after dinner
against the traffic. They had planned

their Revolution and were ready,
their second thoughts told them they were ready.

All that was needed was to wait, to wait
till the Firsts went ahead and had failed;

so the Seconds though ready, waited, secure
in their positions, like people in a book.

Inheritance

The topless native
of our ship trusts
her blue eyes
for she knows already
how this trip will end.

And I half-believe
her, barely doubt
the dog-eared
evidence from a diary
she will publish.

She says it all: she
knows the man I'm
on my way to be. My
predecessors have armed her
with my secrets.

Roots, Roots

My grandmother's donkey had a name
I can't recall. It's not important
for the donkey, a beast of burden
like my grandmother, is dead.
And I am in a different place.

Perhaps the donkey was a horse, a status symbol
or a man, married to my grandmother;
and he lives on with my name.
But then, suppose there was no donkey,
no grandmother, no other place?

Accident

It is no accident
this accident
a lost wife
in the lift
day after day –
the smile today
straying some way past
recognition.
Tomorrow, preened
I shall make
amends. Tomorrow
will our fray
commence. What

if the happy run
of accidents
proves tomorrow
an accident?
I shall curse
the memory; and
when the memory
starts to please.–
I shall be old.

The Kiss

She opened her bag with the scented tissue
And asked for his mouth.
And there in the street she bathed it like her own
For he had been dreaming of her, had tasted her
In that last hour before she was clean.
And the scum of her bath was wiped from his lips
Which left them naked; so she applied the kiss.

A 'Late' Love Poem

He is older, lets
more of it pass: your
flavour

is unique, she says:
a pity to waste it.
He is puzzled

that millions
of uniques
sustaining her

fail to dissolve
into blandness.
There's hope for him, then.

He lets more of it
pass. A pity, she says:
A tragedy

not to have tasted it.

The Lamp

It was a graduation present, she had said –
these ten pieces of wood – all those New York
years ago. We had intended to assemble
it in London, in Stockholm; then in Paris found
that a screw was missing. But we were part
of the house, nevertheless, the one of the future
which would make sense of all these bits and pieces.

Now, rummaging through old boxes to discover
what could be reclaimed, I find our ten
wooden sticks, like a second-hand bargain.
The bestower of our gift is dead, her unspoken
fears long confirmed by everyone but two
stubborn nomads, reluctant to talk about it.
Some boxes later, I find more pieces

of lamp – one of them stamped No. 18. I begin
to accuse the Continents and the years.

An Old Thought for a New Couple

She is not sure
if her failure
was important.

Death strikes
at his eyes again.
He puts on his glasses

and her smile returns.

Village Remains – Old Man

(born c. 1865)

Don't blame me:
when against the run of play
someone scores
let the losing team worry.

You get my meaning.
When the wife
good & true
though generous to a fault
but in all other senses
man of the house,

when she
in breach of custom, dies
leaving me exposed
less-than-half,
the stunted cotton-tree
in a family of weeds –

do you expect a new crop?
The old days back?

Talk of decline had its uses:
here lies the player
who failed the team
still flirting with rules
of the wrong game.
Then graduates came
with theses of Reconstruction.

Now root-gatherers, clearing, prying
discover me here

unrepentant (no hero,
no lost leader in waiting),
the house in ruins,
children's children
precariously abroad.
Don't blame me:
I never was in charge.
Too late by decades
to check diaspora
in the drawing-room
dictionary;

or to mourn a clever half
more safely dead. Indelicate,
really, in a relic
from that house of promise.

Don't Talk to Me about Bread

she kneads
deep into the night
and the whey-coloured dough

springy and easy and yielding to her will

is revenge. Like a rival,
dough toys with her. Black-brown hands in the belly
bringing forth a sigh.

She slaps it, slaps it double with fists
with heel of hand applies the punishment
not meant for bread

and the bitch on the table sighs
and exhales a little spray of flour
a satisfied breath of white

on her hand

mocking the colour
robbing hands of their power
as they go through the motions, kneading . . .
She listens for the sigh which haunts

from the wrong side of her own door
from this wanton cheat of dough
this whey-faced bitch rising up

in spite of her fight, rising up
her nipples, her belly, rising up
two legs, dear god, in a blackwoman's rage . . .

Laughing at her, all laughing at her:
giggling bitch, abandoned house, and Man
still promising from afar what men promise . . .

Hands come to life again: knife
in the hand, the belly ripped open, and she smears

white lard and butter, she sprinkles
a little obeah of flour and curses to stop up the wound.

Then she doubles the bitch up
with cuffs, wrings her like washing
till she's the wrong shape

and the tramp lets out a damp, little sigh
a little hiss of white
enjoying it.

A Little Ritual

I wake you at the right time,
your water ready and bubbling with ash,
the yard smelling of kerosene, the cock too startled to crow.

I let the animal kick me as you slit its throat;
steady it, hold up the lamp
as you scrape it clean, string up and jackripper

like the expert: before daybreak we have meat.
I wash the spot clean of evidence
wash you feed you love you clean of evidence . . .

Now the yard is silent, pig comes
in packets and kerosene lamps went out with you
when the yard died.

And I wash the spot clean of evidence
and love you as you wish
in the past tense.

Nellie in the Bread Room

The lizard scuttling through grass
mocks us both, like a mechanized arm,
or animated toy set to scud
over private memory. This is your room,

the Bread Room, back when the house
was alive. The sky is blue, everyone younger
by a quarter of a century, and you are caught
in a pose we remember: you hold

the flat-iron an inch from your face
to test its heat; and satisfied, make the swap
in the coalpot. The thud thud
of sheets being ironed nails down the stillness

of afternoon into something more permanent
than childhood. Not yet the rumoured thrill
of changing seasons, the promised gift
of snow. Heat: the heat censures

any mood more urgent than restlessness.
From the Animal Pound, greenish-sweet fug
of coalpit soothes like a collective
cigarette. Even the spurt of crowing

from a cock quickly muffles in a flutter
of wings, a scratch of feathers. Mr Frederick,
inching up the hill in time for dinner
will never have to hurry. Now what crawls here

rejects our stale, sea-stained memory
of sweetbread, fruit ripening on trees
named after the family, of freshly-laundered
pride and a piano abusing the afternoon for an hour:

this house, hurricane-proof
built for a free great grandmother
to be born in has served part of its purpose.
Why pick on Nellie's room – one only

of twelve, invisible assets smuggled
abroad to be frozen in a cold country? Time,
left behind, didn't stop there. Like the bookcase
in the drawing-room, whose bindings are too faint

to read; like Ruby, grandfather's horse
surviving him by a decade, or small secrets
of four generations, the House eludes
both us and History. Yet they walk out of your book,

figures from the village coming to fill buckets
at the water-trough, to grind cassava
at the Mill, to bake bread. The ironed cloth
unfolds as Sunday linen on the table inviting

a man with an Irish accent, a vicar, to lunch.
Somewhere, calming a hurricane with prayer,
is grandfather. Everywhere, here, grandmother
presiding over all, too wise to have predicted this.

A History Without Suffering

In this poem there is no suffering.
It spans hundreds of years and records
no deaths, connecting when it can,
those moments where people are healthy

and happy, content to be alive. A Chapter,
maybe a Volume, shorn of violence
consists of an adult reading aimlessly.
This line is the length of a full life

smuggled in while no one was plotting
against a neighbour, except in jest.
Then, after a gap, comes Nellie. She
is in a drought-fisted field

with a hoe. This is her twelfth year
on the land, and today her back
doesn't hurt. Catechisms of self-pity
and of murder have declared a day's truce

in the Civil War within her. So today,
we can bring Nellie, content with herself,
with the world, into our History.
For a day. In the next generation

we find a suitable subject camping
near the border of a divided country:
for a while no one knows how near. For these
few lines she is ours. But how about

the lovers? you ask, the freshly-washed
body close to yours; sounds, smells, tastes;
anticipation of the young, the edited memory
of the rest of us? How about thoughts

higher than their thinkers? . . . Yes, yes.
Give them half a line and a mass of footnotes:
they have their own privileged history,
like inherited income beside our husbandry.

We bring our History up to date
in a city like London: someone's just paid
the mortgage, is free of guilt
and not dying of cancer; and going

past the news-stand, doesn't see a headline
advertising torture. This is all
recommended reading, but in small doses.
It shows you can avoid suffering, if you try.

Over There

Here, when the fresh cut of abuse
falls into an old wound, Over There
comes to the rescue; hot springs & sunshine, the family
putting its head together under a threat,
coming up strong and defiant as Uncle George's laugh,
bruised by malaria in Panama, disappointment in Haiti,
now frozen into myth.

More in respect than grief, parents take to the air.
In the interests of school I am let off
the funeral; but soon learn how Over There
is changing better into best;
is catching God in a good mood
developing and brightening up the place –

though with the old quaking rumble in his stomach
and other crudish side-effects. The great
wild storms of temper still uproot trees
and leave people homeless; but that
is a compromise you can live with: different
here, the grubby hand of hate

setting fire to your house. Can I claim
what they claim, a place so far, its fruit and vegetables
go quaint on my plate, where even footballers
come out playing cricket? Over There
is where parents go to bury family
and come back lighter, for a day or two, bouncing
round the house, as if they're still young.

A Complacent Little Poem
Greets a Revolutionary Big Poem

Listen, think of something else.
The hose is being turned off, blood
washed away; the crowd, numbed
and guilty, won't witness it.

Safe now to write a little poem.
It will face up to the mess,
the broken bodies etc., and hint at something
darker. It will have a fighting title.

Mammie

She would hold up her head though
fresh air still slapped her
about the face
as if she was an immigrant.
She should know better than to gate-
crash at her – now unnecessary –
age, a garden reserved to residents
with a future.
But a little bit of memory returned
to sit with her
to share a past with her
and prepare a joke she could use
against her exile. The ships
which brought them here had seemed
proud and confident, mistresses
of the sea. Now they too
were scrap.
       A familiar wreck adrift
in the city where her husband
went missing, berthed for a moment
like a man from home. She was pleased
he was not the father of her sons.

Penalties

No one is having a breakdown in an upstairs room.
Down here, we accept one another and make
small adjustment to our bodies.
There is one breast missing since last time,

and we fancy we don't know which
without ungallant probing, without disturbing the memory.
At dinner we are unfussy, passing over
the pork, a persistent vegetable, the nearer

of two wines; yet we eat modestly and hope
others take heart from this.
So here we are again – not quite the same
people, but from afar, near enough. Here we are

after twenty years or so, my eyes not quite seeing:
across the table, her fingers in his hair, stranded
without hair. The young wife fills
a gap and does it well. Strange to think that one of us sitting

here is dead. In panic someone will seize
his neighbour and hurry off to make, well, love.
Just in case. And we part thinking ourselves reasonably
in luck. When next we meet another one of us will be missing.

And we are now, older, dreaming of replacements.

The Night of the Short Knives

Suppose then we celebrate:
the scratch on the door at midnight
is now past history. And knives
in the Alley are far from us.

I hear you say: this is an odd
time, a between-the-histories time
for cleaning out attics, clearing
obstacles to restored good fortune.

Let us celebrate again
like survivors rediscovering patterns
in the carpet they have looted: ugly
stains enhance the treasure, after cleaning.

The bowel-moving earthquakes
of the past, twisted metal
of man-made trains and aeroplanes
from which we have escaped, still unsettle

like friends unmarrying themselves.
Suppose we confront the armed man
in the Alley, and claim Right of Theory –
even as we hit the pavement?

The Cost of Sanity

(an English Myth)

We are friends here laying bare
what isn't flesh: we accept
our clothes. Elsewhere
allies defect, leaving gaps in our judgement.
Better to go on meeting like present company.
Better to cover tracks.

This is sanity, not to reach for the world's
blanket of dismay. (In this garden
no one defaults, though I had not thought till now
to hang the mood 'desolate' on this autumn.)
Like friends of long standing, perhaps like strangers
at a party, we can still tease
a phrase that tenses us.

We are in the garden of a friend's home.
Inside, there is famine on a wall. Murder too:
a child, pregnant in a foreign drought. Here, in the garden,
a friend copes, bending to observe what looks like grass:
'Tell me, is it happy? Is the plant happy?'

A Good Day

Her first day out
and about

in the Spring
as promised.

Across the road
a man, his stride unhurried, hands
behind back

handcuffed.
Ah, yes, he knows

his weakness
and today will resist

temptation. No one
is so crude

as to introduce them.

The Sea

It used to be at the bottom of the hill
and brought white ships and news
of a far land where half my life
was scheduled to be lived.

That was at least half a life ago
of managing without maps, plans, permanence
of a dozen or more addresses
of riding the trains like a vagrant.

Today, I have visitors. They come
long distances overland. They will be uneasy
and console me for loss of the sea.
I will discourage them.

3

from Living in Disguise

Haiku

Third-World War

The beach, walking off
inland, dragging its bed of
sand. And look, no guns!

Food-Chain

The feeding over:
one eye hard and accusing –
fish out of water.

Les Chênes du Vilaron

After the concrete
a partner returns to paint
olives on the wall.

Things My Grandmother Never Said

ON LIFE

Don't join the circus:
all you have to protect you
is a safety-net.

ON TEETH

How to say *Xian*?
Your dentist never thought of
travel to China.

Violence on the Tube

Hand on my thigh. Strong
for a girl. Trains make her shy-
ness so hard to bear.

Strange Fish

Then, aware of food-poisoning,
we threw back the culprit disguised
as a fish – and watched

it drown. We cleaned the nets.
Yesterday, we were still watchful
and dumped most of the catch

on waste ground. A gimmick, you say,
with the water teeming.

                  Now, because of pollution,
we must give up fish.

Concessions

A year ago she was a lady
whose husband was travelling,
then she seemed weighed down
by heavy pauses – a winter interlude –
sailboats far from land. Answers
about her mate got lost at sea.

But another year has passed.
Cleverer women confess mistakes
they marvel at, their fury
now directed on those who called them clever;
a few well-meaning armies have turned round
corrupted by television and reporters.

Elsewhere, stray acquaintances have not aged well
this year. A year ago she was a lady
whose husband was travelling,
and she has treated herself to a cure
rigorous as sisters fighting flab.
Now she is fitter, fit

as a sailor rowing towards new land,
as an athlete throwing balls in the air
to mock a rival. Her sky is full
of balloons, brightly coloured like summer
at the resort. A husband sails,
sails on one of them. He's travellin'.

An Old Man Regrets

I should have written a play
for an actress to transform into Ibsen.
Twice in a decade she would come forward, ageless,
and bed me with magic.

Far better than wife.
Wife gets in the way of the madness
driving you up the mountain

to leave a skeleton. Wives, friends
and the less insane grow heavy with waiting
and mist over. And memory,

flickering like candle-light
clears a patch of ground, of sky confusing
past and present. In a youthful country
the woman

buys fresh bread, always cutting into it,
the day before going stale. We fight.
We smother each
country under a blanket of truce.

Now it is all one country.
I should have written travel books
disguised as novels.

I should have given the woman a name.

Arrangement of 95 Words and Their Substitutes

. . . two juvenile leads, performers
on the doorstep after dark, men in jeans
and T-shirts, drawn to the house by cries of murder . . .

In a nearby room the chamber music trio plays (or rehearses)

Up the stairs a man performs upon a woman with his fists.
All play their part: the harm is mitigated
with a coda of understanding . . .

a whiff of chamber music escapes into the air. Goodnight.
When the sun comes up, the still-shapely penitent
paints a gash in the middle of her face:

who are we, today, to tell her how to smile?

Myth, etc.

. . . & in his fortieth year, the sun
rose; no crown of achievement
no broken love-affair

brought this about. He had been prying
open his eyes
since rumour

that a world outside his head
stood there making faces
at him. And what

did he see after centuries
of effort? Mess he didn't recognize
but tried to distinguish

between mine
and *not* mine. He moved to claim all
that was himself

puzzled that it was already used.

4

from Towards the End of a Century

Grandmotherpoem

for grandmother Margaret, 'Miss Dovie', 1867–1953

thinking many things, grandmother
I can't trap the memory, itself like a kite
to blanket us without coarsening our pact:
it is not cold climate, not famine relief that triggers this need.
Though more than the annual hat of fashion must clothe us in
    words.
So I put it off, more and more play the errant;
with dissecting verbs occupy this or that high table where the
    world lies bloated.

You must be asking when this apprenticeship will end?
Running & jumping, ball-games, preaching and Latin were early
    fantasies.
Now, wandering in a garden far from us, I step
on the wrong end of a rake
and crack my skull: the yellow scream of grandmother burns the
    head.
Surprise, a hint of things malordained, skids me past *us*
till embarrassment makes it safe: this is an accident.
A third time I step on the rake: *this is god!* 'Boy, wha happenin?'
I am at risk in the world. This is no accident.
Something leaking through my head has value.
It wines, it lusts, it fills empties fills my space.
Its logic meanders like a stone too heavy for the stream.
It heaves sense against sense cascading down the boneface
while the wet of mothermother drips into thimble: my bucket,
    my ocean.
And the kite is a cloud of badness dribbling, drizzling a parable.
From somewhere maleness spits defiance to hold soft matter in
    its rock of stubbornness
from the wreck, debris of grandmotherpoem
and a thing not recognized as fear of rakes.
Bits of me, long abandoned, floating past

jostle one another like strangers on a march.
The voice which breaks from its full set of teeth
comes like a uniform, polished: we are at risk.
Grandmother, grandmother, her bath over, smelling of bay rum &
    bible
knows how bad habits, like long years abroad, and the profession
    of maleness,
lead to ugly bumps on the head. So men must cover theirs.
In my hat, in a foreign garden, when the leaf is about to fall from
    its tree,
grandmother appears to speak to me:

A Family Gift

I

It must carry no hint of wreath.
The desire that it should be memorable
like that first grown-up party
or going to see the *Lear* formidable
not in ranting on the heath

but in mining tunnels beneath the text's
patriarchy, quelling debate
of mad and sane kings, good and bad daughters
is a rash displaying your own state
of disorder: she's not vexed

by these questions. We agree
something special is in order
for mother's last social outing
like one of us clearing a hurdle, a granddaughter
finally, of exams, breaking free

of a chain of whispers. Now we can display
our private Olympic team of sprinting,
leaping intellect in a Chinese
restaurant – all grandmother's scrimping
and saving rewarded in a way

less mysterious than prayer.
Sorry: let's call truce to these fights.
She will be our visiting dignitary doing
the rounds. Show her the sights,
and promise another tour next year.

She is dressed in black
Smelling of camphor;
Not taking any chances
That she will come back:
So I make a joke about camphor.

Where to go? Art Gallery,
Restaurant or film? Thanks,
You give with one hand
In tradition of the family
And attack with the other: no thanks.

Church is out. Let's not get heavy.
How about a trip south
To an autumn landscape pruned
Of lizards, frogs – *gift-ready*;
And to bring water to your mouth

To bring back the pride of youth
Every kind of grafted mango,
Pear and sugar-apple:
But mother, to tell the truth,
You don't *have* to go.

She never learnt to fly,
Can't put herself through it
Without a cousin, long dead,
Who knew how things worked in the sky
Since no child of hers could do it.

For food and water take
Medicine, matching means to ends;
And secure safe passage from the war,
And good village people to bake
And cook and clean – like old friends.

This is what she asks of children,
And they talk and talk:
She waits growing into dress and camphor,
Thinks: maybe they're not her children,
The way they talk and talk.

III

Too old to start a life, to learn a new address.
Brought here a prisoner or a bride
To this place old and immodest as a man
Gone soft in the head: why do they humiliate me?
Even pages in the Bible look different in this light.
Won't mention it, though; don't want a fight.

The old life is a dream of accident
To family, fire in the street; strangers next door.
This banishment is protection from having again
To witness putting a child's child in the ground
(She traps, spills a memory from the family's old animal pound).
The dog that keeps her company wants to marry; oddly.

So true. And for all his simple tricks
What use is Oskar? He doesn't type or iron or cook.
She laughs at that: why so easy to please?
I revive cancelled outings, *innerthings* over years
Of fastidiousness. Somewhere on the floor
Of my mind, a case not used on recent trips

Holds knick-knacks – a rug from Mexico, jade
From China – possibly for a mother. Awkward, though
Like announcing: today a man first put his foot
On the moon. She's never heard of that, she'd have me know
As if to make the world new again.
And was he family, this Armstrong, was he blessed

By the Reverends Wesley and De Lawrence? Tell me more.
In America a young Irish President – *heard it*
Heard it . . . and two of your sons, Walter and Michael,
Fell off the moon. But uncle Nasser got to Egypt
Not liking conditions on that other canal
In Panama. His house stands empty on our land

Along with others. Bills for repairs will ruin us.
And so they send the boy – always a boy –
From Corinth, from Legba, from Montgomery, Alabama: today,
They will abolish slavery, free the family
To conquer Poland and Russia; to parley
With the Pope – himself related to grandfather.

Though false prophets come with the true
Even here to *Dragon's Teeth*. And now they know
Which Africa is in crisis. Your cousin not long ago
Brought news that Talks somewhere broke down; the humans
Were at fault: abandoned at the Conference, trees
And animals in protest, vowed never to talk again.

And today we are in black, dressed. Our politics
Will not let us admit what this means.
Undelivered gifts will complicate our dreams.
Still, we are conspicuous in the landscape – not as tall
As green above the ground or dead under it.
But clinging to the surface. *Amen*. And aware of it.

Herstory

My name is easy to pronounce, isn't it?
– reward for being young and gliding
towards the heart of the world. History
of a family helped us to travel with travelling
as an option. Though we hoped, by luck,
to arrive somewhere. And after these thirty years'
sojourn, no one will say if this has happened.

Sons seemed designed to ease the travel:
we were young, could produce our own army,
could translate dreams into marks in the dust (a flight
of fancy which warmed some who shuddered in the ship,
      panicked in aircraft).
They say it would take time: we were prepared
better than ancestors. I forget
if they were right. Now, children have grey hairs
and rest between journeys.

And here I am, half by choice, visited
by family. I am at home, they say: others
with difficult names manage exile. My speech
is recognizable; grown men with casualness
of boys call me mother. They do it
eating grapes at my table; without comment working out
riddles at the foot of the bed.

And from time to time something stirs
in them, like the days before they were here
when we trickled in from the edge,
from the foot of a body whose face
was still in the clouds, with words primed to conquer
territory hard as this . . .
Now they come to avenge violence
done to a stranger – that far woman

separated from family; this man – this TV face –
exiled in his own country, hospitalized,
yet young enough to be photographed, for love
to have the old meanings . . .
Their freedom is what these children
half-strive for. They are skilled in grand
impossible names, not like mine.
Too late for me to dissent. But children
have children: there's comfort in that.

This England?

. . . guests at midnight
. . . guests at midnight stopping
outside the house. The one
without the gun demands

her name and (through
an interpreter) tells Mammie

she's got nothing to fear
if she's legal.

Love Song

And they promised her fire instead of ice
And now last of the brothers comes
For her to melt him

Stone
Wall
Brick

Against her song
This man
Last of the twins

His stone
His wall
His brick

Surviving the body-language of a Sister
Will melt
Under her song

Song about the bell
The fire-
Engine

She is fire-engine
She is bell
From her mouth new sounds

Of metal, furnace, engine
(Not her sounds)
Of boardroom, office, platform

And her face
Is bruised
From the argument

Refusing to change shape
Temperature
The lover

Intact
Traps her metaphors
Into a grammar of ice

And it is so foolish
To train bells and fire-engines
On her own fire

Rewrite

Beauty screws her new
leg into place and gains
advantage. Blame the limp,
she says, on Progress: who's
for a game then?

for a game then? I'll play,
let me play, says the Beast
sick of being upstaged again.

The hoof in the chest –
a new experience to Beast –
puzzles him: for so long
it had been *his* rôle to give
those beauties pleasure.

Nibble, Nibble

All these yuppie orphans, eager
to be fed – damn,

d'you mind? She removes
the blouse stained

with drink or food
from an OK country:

no guilt there, you see?
As I always say,

can't be too careful
about things these days . . .

as competing mouths nibble
nibble at the tips of

there there . . . strawbooby
nutsy-wutsy whatsits

from a new garden.

Love in the Hospital

She slaps him; feels a twinge:
and now he won't hit back. Too weak
to stamp hot anger on her face
he heaves, heaves. She slaps him
perhaps to hurt
more than pride: through blood
and memory he sees her peeling
cardigans, wife-flesh collapsing
heaps in front of strangers.
The shame of it. Nurse. Nurse!
She struggles to remove shirt and trousers
skinning him naked in reproach.
There is no blood. Nurse holds the eye
of an ancient ally, draws back, colludes.
In seconds she has banished
old age, marriage, from her plans.
The other has not lived for this:
this is no payment for life's
submission – though she must return
compliments she was never meant to have.
She slaps him not for the ward's
benefit; and there, damp soft
clay she can't quite mould
through years of fingers going stiff;
and it hurts, the pressure hurts.

The Mother's Tale

So many terrible people are people still
— GAVIN EWART

Goodness, she said:
Unless you eat this,
Unless you get to bed

The black man
Will get you
And that's worse than

Being dead.
You're all at sea now
In above your head:

The grasping hand
Reaching out to you
From land

Is folly. Just realize
I didn't make you try that one
For size.

He's everything
I promised
Though he won't sing

And dance.
And if he doesn't beat you, well
That's by chance.

I'm truly sorry for being right
Though we must take
Delight

In the buff-
Coloured darlings. Yes,
It's been rough

For all of us,
Determined to meet this setback
Without fuss.

We've been here before
With the Wars and bullies:
It's just a bore

In a home like this
To have brought on
With the bedtime kiss

When this game began
Something rather worse
Than the stock policeman.

The Thing Not Said

We need life-jackets now to float
On words which leave so much unsaid.

How can this not sound like sophistry
To justify absence from your thoughts, your bed?

But this haemorrhaging of language
Still keeps the best phrase locked in my head.

Easy to talk of loneliness, of ageing, damning
Those who would be Presidents and Generals of the dead;

Forgetting the detail, the particular hunger
Of someone you know waiting to be fed.

And now I'm doing it again, drifting on words,
More lines for the simple thing not said.

5

from Letter from Ulster
& The Hugo Poems

Hinterland

The dreams are wet. Tonight rain
In Portrush, home of two months. I wake
To seagulls, accept the logic
Of dream and unpack the cases: life
Will be here near Malin Head –
Like Rockall, an outpost on the weathermap.
I rehearse a prayer to my travelling
Relic, a grandmother sure to exact,
Like other gods, penance for this blasphemy.
The first wet dream was not the joke
Schoolboys brag about, but fear
Of stretching out a foot from Montserrat
And falling into sea. In France, in Germany,
In spray-white Sweden the first stumble
Across a street turned ground to water
With waves of language rearing up
To lift you out of depth. Lucky
You didn't unpack – though the cases now
Are full, wares and gifts outdated,
And your fresh discoveries changing shape
And colour like your photograph.
Another day in Portrush: wind and rain.
There is security in this, part
Of the hinterland of an experience
Still to be reclaimed. New Guinea
Was too fabled, generous in its reprieve:
A threat – its gift too close to dreams
For waking comfort. London was like a parents'
Home from which to rebel. Now here, on the edge
Of the edge, the sea hurling defiance
At old, at new gods, I pray to the familiar
In my suitcase, in my head: I have
Explored the world, tasted its strangeness,
Resisted and colluded out of strength,

Out of weakness, failed to colonize it
With family tongue or name. Are you pleased
Secretly, with a frown pulling down on relief?
The treasures I carry in my head fail
To match the refuse in my case.
But it will do, and the dreams tonight
To douse a fear, will perhaps be wet.

Island

1

A convenient image only
to help you, my friend, my darling,
my destroyer – and talking of destroyers,
white and splendid on the sea,
like forbidden triumphs of an early
culture, hermaphroditic in their promise,
Ladies growing erect with guns – enough.
Enough to bring the blush to past lovers.

2

Do not mock the poverty of our invasion,
mis-spelled placards and voices which parody
sound, thanks to your friends – so powerful
they need no uniforms – who have held us
from the presence. Don't be generous;
do not arrange a delegation through
the cordon. You know what's written there.
My love, you know also, most of these wrecks
which disturb your peace, are sunk. Unsafely.

3

'He survived the plane-crash.'
These are the ones who didn't,
and have torn through the skim
of our life to remind us
of the myth. The day your logic
broke and you stuck it together
and no crack showed through the sentence,
is being remembered, is being lived.
Those for whom cracks were never mended
are here, bits of them trying to assemble
bits of you they care to claim. They attack –
guns, bombs, badverbs – evacuated arguments.
On the horizon, another island afloat, Ah,
in a sea of salt: a line,
a rope, a plan of rescue:
how best to invade?

I'm Looking through Glass, I'm Tasting Poison

1

I'm searching, searching for a first line
as if chained to the bed, unthinking you . . .
I'm washing the bottoms of milk bottles, prior to fridge.
I'm thinking of timeless gestures – the cat darting in, out
as the door ends centuries of waiting.
These memories mist the glass too easily:
Better to look through it, and think of others tasting poison.

2

And as I talk to myself again through you,
knowing you're unlikely to have names and faces
I imagine; or, in a darkened theatre
a blur from up here, behind lights –
there is no need to play it safe, to match
halves for the perfect fit tonight.
So, behind glass, I plunge into Sahara. I swim.

3

I am blind, of course, the glass
is a trick of sight. Eyes
glaze from footage on the assembly line
like the years passing in stanzas, inches from my face,
regiments of maimed, the undead to make me see.
I see: then how better to use this magic
to quell let's call them furies, too much explained?

4

Let's say there is grief, or something less
too tempting to indulge. Let's say
on a body that side of glass, a scar
reforms into the healing smile of Second Best.
How can you retain faith in the old storms,
the kind raging in the head, flooding
your own country, silting its river?

5

I lower my guard as if you're here beside me:
we've hung the pictures, reordered the room
for living. Through the window your fingers bloom
like flowers new to my vocabulary. The glow
of your voice outliving the piano flickers
what might have been . . . might have been.
The rest is silly. The drink is funny.

6

I lower my guard as if you're here beside me –
the pretence of talking in public dropped –
the fart, in pride, restrained as you come in to tease
flowers new to my vocabulary into season,
far from assembly-line of days to remember days
to regret. And we vow, don't we, to recover what is ours
by exxing out those lines about glass and poison.

from Letter from Ulster

for Mimijune

1

I'm 300 years old;
the partner arrives and is shown into
the drawing-room where someone makes her comfortable.
She is, we think, 40 years early.
The boy sits in an upstairs room, his back
to the window, typewriter on the bed
two-finger tapping a scene from the house
next-door – a young girl folded in the arms
of a man, open curtains with promise
that travel from St. Caesare to Ladbroke Grove
might fulfil. Neither typist nor writer he turns
too late, the curtains are closed.
Downstairs, mother entertains an in-law 40 years early
with scenes from a life more real than this:
the drawing-room floor is freshly polished, smell
of wax like flowers from the garden toasting
in the sun. Wasps' nests have been removed
from gable and gallery, lizards and other irritants
dealt with by someone unseen who nurses
a better version of this house. Look out
of the window – through glass panes, a bridal
present for the young mother never to shed
hint of girlishness in the crossing – glass panes,
first on this side of the island –
at grapes with a hint of salt, though the sea,
as you see – so calm today, how could we be sick? –
is distant . . . ah. But will you take
ginger beer or coconut juice with ice? Downstairs,
in this recent house imposed on other houses where occupants
vanish in mid-sentence leaving you unsure of tricks
being played – downstairs, brothers talk of an election

coming up, promises that must be made
to us here in England, to us in South Africa,
to us everywhere as price of the vote. (Old Professeur
Croissant used to say in class: if you must lie,
lie intelligently. If you must, sell yourself
dearly, a play on words too risky for parents born
before our time.) Excluded from the couple
behind their curtain and from the brothers' debate
– and from what else? – I plead
unreadiness to meet a partner, years early.

2

Dear X,

They call it confidence to offer
false starts to an intimate this late
in the game, but what if no better version comes? . . .
though this stand colludes, perhaps, with failure.
So, dear X, skip these lines of self-
regard, worn apologies
for omission, unreadiness, these practised
ways of shoring *Self*. To you, to others
who have turned up early, these games
irritate; they bore. Mock the time
with family growing into the real thing.
Stray postcards confirm your luck, you've escaped
the jokes – remember when Pullar and Parkhouse
were in contention to open the batting for England? –
that no one understands. That off our chests – Oh chest! –
safe to revert to the present with a letter
from Ulster. Scenes of local colour
won't do the trick – too much blood
under the lamp-posts, joke. 300 years seems
a short time to manage a life cleansed
of its past yet love-propelled;
but my time-creditor comes like an assistant

at the bank and says, enough: others,
who are not bright, manage it in the slot
allotted. Think of lives you have put
on hold by slowing things to this pace. Your drawing-
room partner, distanced now by – whom? – a stand-in
daughter, has outlived the house, the fantasy.
Brothers, far from downstairs, answering to other
cares protect themselves from new 'South Africas'
(child and wife and self-abuses, biologies with your name
on). And they go out to vote. And what, pray,
of that early couple behind the curtain?
But I promised you relief from a letter
too stiff to compel reading between
the lines. A limp letter, then, and addressed
to someone, on another continent, not tempted
to read between our lines.

Dear Jim & Elisabeth,

This is not the letter, I know. I'll write
at the weekend to thank you for Canada
(lovely present, unspoilt, where will I put it?)
for good times remembered, the walk through the ravine
that beautiful Sunday with Elisabeth (we're adults now,
no Atwood childhood fears. Remember Cat's Eye?)
Thanks for the hospitality, the space . . .
But first, let me clear my mind a bit
as resolution ebbs on this Coleraine-Belfast train.
Cutting it fine, as always, I crash the guardsman's
van, pleased, no seconds today, to spare –
and I'm missing a package, a bag – left
in the taxi, snatched on the steps? the race
over foot-bridge, messy: students pouring the other way
helped when the straps broke: white bag
with books, green bag MADE IN CANADA, my change
of clothing, a white top, for Belfast,

after a bath – fresh for the late-night studio.

I'm in the guard's van. Maybe he thinks:
they need longer to recover breath
than men in our parts, all that running and jumping
on television. He makes small allowances
for this puffing race and settles a little more
in his skin. Today, bag-snatched, I see no reason
to take better care of his feelings than he does.
I rise to the occasion (it's a coarse time
but we'll outwit it) and see hoardes cross the bridge,
motorcycle-helmeted, moll-painted, struggling
to don white Westing House gear and I . . . check myself in time.

Dear Elisabeth & Jim

3

A government-suited man behind a desk: to show
he's human or to ease the tension, makes a joke
(not about the Chinese lady at Dhu Varren
railway station, though that comes to mind) . . . Which of us
will act this man's throwaway line
and end up in the papers? And here we are coming out
of the film of the book, telling friends over a pizza
how the cut-price Bogart got it wrong. Across the road
filmed, too, in drizzle your tail lights a cigarette in the doorway.
   See!
Better to talk about the railway clock in Portrush Havishamed
at 11.25 encouraging old bachelors
to rewrite their history as literature.
I've caught the bug. Let me read you
the menu of the Chinese restaurant
(Lower Main Street) as a poem . . .

You're right, my love. The act
degenerates, distraction/from a life

we might have lived/points
to an analyst

behind this glimpse of happiness,
behind this naked breast, voices
of old men unscramble/made human
by translation, their toothless lives no longer
excluding from the feast of family feeling
those not dressed for table:
the rhubarb chorus (something to rhyme with table?
to swat the buzzing chorus?)
makes you pause and turn away/careful
not to repel the naked breast/I say
having lost the prize:
I will add some years to mine

till it comes around next time.

4

Meanwhile enter Horace
our Interlude, pink
ribbon in his hair, pink
shoe-lace in his memory-
pocket for a daughter
ever pink and beautiful:
Derringer's the name
name o'th'game, our Shaman
restored to humour.
Wars & roaming have dis-
tempered, slack-minded
this lover of Peace, stiff-
limping into action.
He appears on cue
against the tide of Comanche Cheyenne Sioux
back to you (he can do
the Ali shuffle, too!):

now at his piano miming
the old tunes. *In The Mood*
& If I Give My Heart To You . . .
(10,000 at Salamis, more at Zama
negotiations between the generals having failed)
Will You Handle It With Care . . . ?
He is not blind, he outwits
doctors and family, this Special
Envoy to Europa, bringing *shhh*
(from St. Caesare, off
your map, don't look now)
Bustcrumvrst Mvst
Peace in his language,
in this or that language:
Messenger Horace broken-
toothed on his diet of phrases
WIR HABEN (try this one)
UNS MIT NACHBARN ÜBER DIE
BENÜTZUNG DES GARTENS ARRANGIERT
no pillow-talk now to Merles
& Sadies of Coderington
to Cathy and Sharon of Ealing and Edmonton.
But public lament for
Hrothvitha Hrothvitha
stage-wife and daughter
petals in the slaughter
to divert you from comfort,
from solemnity. And so –
May you never lack for caress
May your lover be left-
                    handed and relentless
May Sally paint your door in bright colours
May you be the pick of your brothers
and so on and so on *Hrothvitha*
Hrothvitha a name no one claims for
these Sisters and Mothers.

Brokentoothed fly-
opened Horace ends
with a memory that he sings
unaccompanied, his own melody, pink-
ribboned melody, his
something-hearted melody, his
broken-charted melody, his

broken-hearted melody . . .

5

Puck
Just a note, darling;
I've had to explain you
appropriate you (for Mimijune &
Julieblossom) to see how you'd run:
Ama Ata Aidoo,
triple A.
b. Ghana, 1939, playwright,
novelist, etc. Address Zimbabwe
(see essay by Innes,
Lyn of Canterbury). So,
you were my near-choice
for the Chair
to prick these Oberons,
these Titanias (immune with collars)
and constituencies cross-
border (swing high, swing low . . .)
with a virus of compassion
as they learn to betray your name
in a common accent:
Ama Ata Aidoo
Chairperson to this Conference
not allowed
(by a daughter of Ghana,
sister of Zimbabwe)

to break up
on this rock of malespeak
solid through the ages.

Mimijune, Julieblossom.
In the wings. My favourite things.

6

I wake up howling: murder
has become easy to the long-lived. I'm committing
it again. The pistol in the pants
slugs a consenting victim
in the crotch. I do not have Aids,
I say. But the victim dies. Everywhere
it gets easier to kill. (And the coward
says: let me turn away from the loved one
before we wake.) Meanwhile the years
turn against us. Solutions elude us.
How long, O Lord, is this string spun
from vanity, how long
will the earth sustain it?

Dear John & Joan,

(lacking courage
for today again on the television, an outrage
occurs – the plumber, shop-assistant outguesses
me in the quiz of what I call my subject.
Pride must be recovered before approach
to another with intent.
Lacking courage like
the blind man at Sheffield Railway Station
charging down the stairs, scattering passengers;
like getting on with a former life;
like dying early, I turn
to another, slack letter, my darling,

and mild abuse of Canada. In lieu of lovers'
cards, the codes uncracked in the post,
I blame the time, I blame the place.)

My mispronunciations of Agincourt were deliberate.
I, too, live in Henry V country only when abroad.
Just a letter from Ulster to thank you for Canada,
big country, clean accent, etc . . . And about me?
O, fun times in Ballymena, Ballymoney. Limavady.
Riding the middle of the train one day (not the first
carriage or the last, making it safe, like a New Yorker
story shorn of beginning and end) the second smoker
lights up, the third girl-farmer splotches mud on my seat:
I like it, folks, the wild North, I'm not too late
for the rush. Later, I'll play myself in Hollywood.
But competition is stiff for the films. At audition
near Portrush (the place where the train, programmed
to leave late, surprises you one day by being early)
I rated one line, the privileged extra . . .
The time is evening, the place Dhu Varren, the train
not running. A bus – looking like a bus – pulls up
and rail-passengers get on. Except for the Chinese
lady hovering, holding out. 'There's no train today';
the conductor treads on my cue, with no result.
The language-student wants a playback. So pointing
to UNIVERSITY *bus, idling, he announces:* THIS IS
THE TRAIN. *This, a week after events at Tiananmen*
Square where nobody died. This 'train' an English
joke in Ireland?

Old men used to say: stones grow.
Men at home grew grey on such evidence.
No one thought of land-erosion. But the same men say:
cut me and I bleed, auditioning for Shylock;
trapped here, I die. Ah, if they thought of land-erosion
they would find ways out of this, with the family intact.
I stand accused of lengthening moments

into string, as if that were in short supply
in the average life.

> *O yes, I meant to say, they sent me*
> *a list of 24 poets, names and addresses,*
> *colleagues at the HARBOURFRONT, for a week. Telephone*
> *numbers, too. How open. How good. Canada.*

Mimijune, Julieblossom,

The change of clothing, the white top
reclaimed at home in Portrush, my oversight,
made me see how rash to write too soon
a letter from Ulster, to write to you
in innocence. Instead, the white top,
stolen on the road from London to Sheffield,
delays the letter. But what of you?

7

Portrush: Fragments from the Journal

I

Land, I think, though only just.
Gales from Iceland whistle through the caravel.
The seas, enraged at this obstruction threaten,
relent and come again, green-backed with teeth
straining from the world of myth. Some say
these monsters will not be ridden; these are tales
of desperate men far from home. Next will come
the triumph of supping with the devil
without the long spoon; and that will grant your wish
of keeping good folk at home.

II

Then the land shrank back in a terrible roar
As the green-backed, white-teethed
Mass made for the shore
Spitting sea-pebbles with venom
Like a line of snipers compelling
You to yield. This zealot's canon
Bends you down, crouches you in mime
Of humans in drink, each desperado
– And we have all been there in time –
Fantasising a railway-station pub at Portrush.
And some say the King of Spain
Has now laid claim to Portrush.
But on to the real El Dorado round
The promontory, our university teeming,
Its band of natives browned
By no sun, and like the bless'd of the old
World, well-proportioned, except for webbed
Feet and tendency to walk backwards in leave-taking. Gold
Is our currency, though rival discovery
Of men with breasts or bird or fish aspect
Still serves, if not national recovery
Or fixing the State plumbing,
To head off ruin and the Tower. The *cassique*
In chains, must fear our Second Coming.

III

Too dangerous to say what you've found.
The sealed envelope (why should this be found?)
Would explain all should we suffer mishap.
A new god of hail descends like an icecap
Sneezing; unkind to flesh and eyeglass. Wind & rain
(And faulty instruments) make it hard to retain
Our humour. Exploring's no longer the sum
Of delights promised when the journey was begun.

Wet with indignity, men think this train
Of misery that brought them here, the same
That through Law of Averages, if not prayer,
Must lug back to those early stations of hope. Fair's fair.
In time a train train stops unscheduled at Portrush
Where the spirits have not been propitiated. Portrush
Is a rooftop vandal hurling down slate at your feet
Daring you to assume safe passage to Main St.
You get home bleeding, fire-water the graze
And much else; relent, and sit down to write the day's
Journal when the light blows out.
I'm sitting in the dark; there are Christians about.

J'accuse

We did all the right things
Worked all the week
Treated the servants well
Added to the house, praised
Those spirits who didn't embarrass us.

Some turned cane into sugar,
Into rum: we were lucky
With cotton. And at night
When the hill-side god deserted
Our stone foundations and spare rooms,

And set the animal pound braying,
And the kerosene lamp flickering,
We recited the old stories
Of hurricanes fought in these rooms
With bibles white and black

Through to a safe morning.
But what to do about gods
Gone missing, asking forgiveness
From this or that far land,
Their protection

Like the mosquito-net, an upside-
Down catch for fish, a mockery,
As the days wear their night-
Games, servant and mistress standing in
Remagicking the house

As cassava-box melts into
Coffin, black against white
Poison (and the carpenter, maker

Of box and coffin, at rest, somewhere,
Innocent)? We did the right thing

For we had paid already
With children in the ground,
And men who hadn't written,
And men who repaired the wrong house.
Now, long after we're gone, a ship

Crashes into our mountain,
Its people uninvited, reclaiming
Cassava boxes, soon to be blessed.
Hard to found a village, even now,
With so much sacrifice.

A Poem about a Savant, a Sister & a Person very Grand at a Function who must first Look around the Room for Someone more Important to Talk to, and then Relent.

He was the Stapleton who matured
like cheese which reminds you of something else
into a Character the village loved
to offer to strangers as evidence

of a sophisticated palate. Old Stapleton
talked calmly of violence and death
unlike the preacher, to banish both as a daily fear
without condemning the island to something folksy.

He preserved the risk that he could do worse
if he tried, to confirm the family's dread
of *savant* as something others called strange
in whispers or with after-dinner relish.

Though for a sister, visiting,
how irksome this man without family
making death 'n violence a party piece, neighbours
she'd kept at bay by effort in a life

ministering to others! And here they are together
at a function, approached by a person very grand,
contrition on his face. And yes, women
are like wives to public men at times like these.

Old Stapleton tells the story of his sister's
daughter when young, helping to pull weeds
from the driveway, from the garden: why then
is she crying, the happy child? Those flowers

in an adult hand, though green, have done no harm,
and calling them names won't make it better.
This story of death and violence in the family
softens the sister and intrigues a person very grand.

On Explaining the Result of the Race to your Mother

Her eyes are bad; you can't take refuge
in that: her sons erect on the podium
receiving medals for running and jumping
have to be acknowledged. Why *them*, you think,
with a rash of jealousy lotioned
into something more presentable: *they*
chasing the wind, leaping the bar, have stretched
your mind, too, past comfort. So why not us, nearer
home, greyer, trailing in another pack but clutching
goodies made visible by our words? The old arguments
are too heavy for mind alone to shift. Three sons
(not strangers), same face, accent, each with a national
anthem not her own: the mother's eyes
see past this snub. There were times, it's true,
when men left home to build in foreign
lands, and scattered seed where no one knew.
A few decades reapprenticed to the world and we've shifted
view on what's good and not good to know; there are
no bastards in this family now grown large
by claiming its own. But the flags
held aloft by children fingering medals
have nothing left of our cloth: will this extend
the emergency order of exile? A memory
fogs like cloud over those factories, farms unkind
to animals which bring protesters out on the street.
Ah yes. But remember, the sky over cruelty
can be blue: (so many flags show good weather!)
Let's watch the television; your distant sons
smile and wave. Daughters now. More flags. Gold
hung from necks more precious than the rest. And let's
not look at one another while we're being honoured.

Death in the Family, 1988

after a father, for a mother

1

thinking about my mother, thinking
about a joke she might have told, setting
the scene to make it seem

unforced . . . The butcher's shop in Ladbroke Grove in the '50s
was a tough audition for one
unaccustomed to playing the messenger, or head of the family:

there, weighing need and status –
heads and tails and innards ruled out;
dead flesh to be cleaned ruled out –

bits of chicken, then, one bit for each member
for this is England and exile made you measure
not only the weight of glances and words thrown across the street

but what you ate
and how much warmth you let into the air around you:
five bits of chicken, please.

The telephone rang and rang and guilty
to be caught at this after 30 years
I learnt of a death in the family.

I listened to what accompanies news of death in the family,
and promised to pass it on,
and agreed how it should be passed on

And I checked myself for signs of afterlife.
The bath this morning to greet the world
seemed right; panic about bills unpaid began to subside.

The damp-marks in my room still sent the same message.
REPAIR ME.
Estrangement from a too-dear friend, her beauty flawed
in wanting to embrace the cheat in you –

seems less like logic now, less
like damp marks on walls, less like
your shift within the world.

For now, my son, a quiet hand has removed
a shelter that was useful, that was kind (why
aren't there hurricanes, revolutions, strange happenings as in *Lear*?)

There is nothing between you and the last appeal:
you are pressed against the barricades; the space
which cushioned till today, is occupied by you now:

you can't decline it, choice remains
but like a shadow to your self
like the two-headed coin you toss without protest: you must take

the weight of others
who will not grant breathing space
who look at you as fixture, always there

who are impatient, reckless, sporadic in their need
who want sometimes to fail – to check if you are real
who do and do not wish to take your place

and I go to the bathroom and find that things work much the same
and I suspect countries on the map are where we left them
and I welcome the shy, unexpected, prod of hunger . . .

2

I think back to that '50s scene
the lady (wife, long-distanced, to the one
whose death is now reported: we will tell her, we've discussed it)

losing her tongue, like a novice, at this butcher's shrine
(she knew a husband's commandments would be obeyed).
Later, it was possible, when chicken came in bits –

not that they came in bits, you understand: that was
the joke that never worked – later, in another part of town
when she had grown attuned to shopping

(but not to taking insides from dead meat)
she developed ways of withstanding
the pressure of the queue – and of honing her joke.

Five pieces not because there were five in the family
– there were five in the family –
but because in this England you had to count things differently.

From this they understood much
that she had not intended:
even the jokes here set you back.

Another failure, the family, growing tired of wings
made their own jokes of being tired of wings:
five legs seemed so difficult to be at ease with . . .

Thinking back to what produced five legs
she saw two of her mother's chickens *and a half*.
The horror of the half made her think

in this long-frozen land
where the family, itself a half of something never planned,
this was a joke all would understand:

so she asked for *five* pieces from two chickens
and a lame one; and the man with blood on him laughed . . .
When she moved house again the other man laughed.

A Little Bit of our Past . . .

for Olive and Jessica

Here's a bone under glass, and reproductions
of birds long vanished known to ancestors
who wouldn't have imagined us. Other exhibits show
birth, marriage and death, their dry riverbed
of history, moistening with recognition
that the cultivated areas where we live
are not far from the source. Closer still,
the soundtrack lifelike, the dress modern, a mother
beating her son with inherited skills
some in our midst claim to possess.

The mother – call her Olive, call her Jessica –
a petite, kind woman you'd treasure
as a friend, asks you to witness her problem.
This is no big Momma beating up on the boy,
but a priestess of manners ordained to prevent
Satan re-entering the family as an animal.
He so rude he drive you to distraction.
Here she is all dressed up and ready to go out,
he not just making her late he spoiling her style, daring
her to use whip as if she's some marketwoman
anxious to parade herself in public. What to do now?
She don't even have a strap to teach the boy a lesson.
So she have to fold up her little fists into a ball
and shut her eyes tight not to see as she thump him up;
and he hurt her hand, you know?
And now the exertion make her hot; she flush, she have
to go change her blouse again, and sprinkle
a little water on her skin to cool it down –
and don't talk to her about shame and humiliation and feeling small:
You know something just spring loose inside her head
which make her mad. The boy lips curl up like a challenge
from on high, *and it make her mad!*

And you know she can't even remember if he start to throw
back words at her, but she hearing them.
The more she hit and cuff, the more she bathing him in licks,
she feeling the blows, she taking *Language* in exchange
that lash and sting and curl her up; she feel
those sudden jets of steam that catch you from the kettle, bruising
    her.
The way he standing she knows the boy still aiming
words at his mother as if this is boxing-
ring, and he squaring up against his equal.
And he jabbing her with rudeness like
he is big man already playing with woman.
And if you witness such a scene no one could say
she don't have duty as a Christian and a woman
to teach him manners –
it's her cross to bear and everyone must suffer in this life.

And Maisie used to say: you got to beat them till
they say sorry and they mean it,
which is not a lot to ask of people who are not beasts of the field:
some say you have to start early
before they turn into man like the men already in your life,
ready to walk all over woman and cause trouble in the land,
and, you know, the sorts of arguments that go with that.
But child, I don't believe it doing any good,
whether you beat him in his Sunday clothes
or on the nakedness too raw and proud for comfort now,
is you going suffer pain, till they relieve you.
For licks not going to stop woman liking him
which is what you fear and hope;
and in the end you tired and beaten –
and you compromise and ask the boy the hurtful question.
You look him in the eye and say: why it is you want to kill me so?
And if I tell you that the child so rude and stubborn
he refuse even to answer, you going say I lie!

A Date on the Calendar

The days come and go.
I lurch this way and that
through my Amazonian
exile, dripping

hallucinating. I get up,
peel away nightrags,
find something dry,
uncontaminated

and collapse again.
Dreams come in shoals,
jealous of body's treat
to something special;

or to collude with brain
that minutes not days
break these spasms
of measurement.

I dream a man
remote from us –
a white farmer, say,
somewhere in Africa,

or Wyoming –
calls on a lady
of my acquaintance. She buys
(or sells or declines)

a ticket for a function.
She marks the date
on the calendar. Ah,
the rest is forgotten.

I am travelling down
Orinoco, hacking through
Yanamami country. Centuries
or inches. Time to take stock.

Bodyrags cling to me.
How could you sieve
so much sludge
through unbroken skin

and be repelled
by a life of slime?
You grasp a bramble:
African farmer

and Wyoming lady
resolve their bet.
One wins. The other chooses
a date on the calendar

to oppress me. Us.
And here I am
becoming fish.
Here I am

Letting old rivers
of salt bed me,
unable to change
for the wedding.

Maurice V.'s Dido

1

'Over the bulwark into the sea
that's where fair Dido has transported me.'
But we soon moved on from that, boys
at the Grammar School, taking cue
from Maurice V. – not The Fifth, not King
of St. Caesare, despite his titles, just the sharp turn
of our year & first to call her Dido, our Queen
some years divorced from the Latin class
(*urbem quam statuo, vestra est; subducite naves*).

She was Queen of France to those ignorant
of Carthage, daughter of Maas Charlie who lost
face and partner in Guadeloupe and prospered his charge,
not yet Queen, torment of our dreams,
on an estate he overseered or owned
with family settled abroad. There were grown men about
who swore 'Princess' Miss Geraldine was worth
bobbing on the Montserrat ferry this way
piled with provisions, that way with goats and live chickens
for . . . *Dido herself, splendidly beautiful* . . .

though not yet *widow*, married
or *giving way to frailty* as we think,
except as token for a quick boy
soon to leave the island on high tide of scholarship.

So we were willing fodder for Maurice V.,
old *heathens* from Coderington, skilled
at defying the adults, parents, aunts
on Sundays and in hot dreams escaping from our pants.

2

So boys, says Maurice V. wearing his crown
as 'Village Idiot', a title volunteered
to old Mister J. who asked one day in Physics
about professions after school expecting the usual
Doctor, Lawyer... Nurse, maybe – Got to be serious now:
we can't go give her majesty fair arms
except to complicate this business of colour.
Got to set an example here, to show those bitches in power.
After that, 'fair' Dido seemed too *period* for this reign
even to dull boys in 5b agreeing out of shame.
(So that's why I going board she like pirate: *bam*).
... Most desired ship in our harbour, Dido,
the Lady who promised transport
to Medicine, the Law and other foreign spoil,
finds a boy rude against her waterline ... These words
are ladders in the stocking of her frailty
gaining us the decks ... *Now:*
Most desired ship in our harbour, Dido ...

So what you think? Maurice V. asks as Ivan
and Pewter and Everton playing cool now the real Everton
has toured and spent the afternoon coaching –
What you think? he asks
one night at Sturge Park after the match
where we were beaten by some country team literal
about games; and we all agreed, advisors now,
that with the power of diction,
with a scholar fierce enough to dig up ground
when passing water, and with more than Virgil
and Shakespeare to rifle for language – the *bulwark*
image which he coined after hooking
that boy for six and losing the ball, reflected
browsing browsing, man – and with us
to keep the metaphors smashing back and forth, 'stocking
of her frailty', nothing special: our nerve holding,

Maurice V. stood chance with the overseer's daughter
where others – from ancient Libya & Tyre
and now the blue-jacket man from Hither Gaul –
failed; failed bad enough to *bawl*.

3

All who had failed, failed here.
St. Caesare, spread out, was a map of the world's
battlefields, from ancient to modern to now.
Last week's Irishman from the sea minus a hand: what made
him so generous to fish with bait that had caressed
maybe foreign, cool and freckled women in lace
but *sickness* for our grape-coloured Geraldine?
On Sundays, squaring up to hymns long learnt, uncles,
more by courtesy than blood, surviving Panama
and Haiti showed breaches in the mouth, no trap
for Geraldine, a 'dentist' harder to please than all Trujillo's
henchmen, armed with parsley
teaching foreigners a lesson in pronunciation
on the massacre river that night in '37
demanding your life for your accent. Survived to mock
neat stanzas like schoolboy graffiti in the margin
of the hymnal, of bats with human organs, the wife of X
bubbling rudeness to old Mister J., 'pallid' as the shade of Sychaeus
– parsleytenors seem to shout: with these flares she'll see us.
(I can hear them: *And with these flares she'll see us . . .*)

Agnosco veteris vestigia flammae . . .
But the Queen was not a night-scholar
in this language gone stale in our climate:
you know what going happen if I not careful?
she asked her suitor, granting him a drink
he'd never tasted, letters behind his name, foreign
travel (he wished she had a loyal sister to act
as prologue or else, saving her, cue his play).
He proclaimed her soulmate not needing

him to be best at this or that, just sharpest
at the commentary, 'bed-pressing', boy (you so fresh
& *rysche*) like no mere text-
book swot but a *browser* with wit
to counter Ivan's height and Pewter's claims
to family letters going back beyond grandparents
(handwriting legible, spelling good): he quelled
his fear that she saw *through* him
a stranger in a jacket made to sail
ships to fly planes, rich in imported
je ne sais quoi lines from Racine, Molière,
a few bars of Piaf . . . would this suffice for indifferent
gods – like Messrs. Wesley & De Lawrence – to see him through?

To woo or not, like a tailor or seamstress, on his knees,
was the question: how else to match lips
to lips that were too knowing? He would bribe
the gardener, groom, whatever, the stand-in Punic Noble;
cram the names of flowers new to love:
how right this clematis matched her present mood!
Dido herself, splendidly beautiful, purple-hued,
(wilful enough to flirt the old school uniform, hair tied up in
      braids)
was saying to Maurice V.:

So you want to make
soup with me, dasheenman, is what you take
me for? maybe you just hate
me deepdown, eh? . . . like you
come come rumour me, you want
to put hoe in my hand . . . or cutlass, maybe: you men
are all the same; why you don't go spray your energy
in foreign bush where your mind is already,
and stop stinking up the ground? Relieved
to be a man, relieved that this was Geraldine still,
raw in the mouth and not some distant Colette
or Yvette raised, portcullis-like, in Paris

beyond yards of snow (though prune-coloured
language on a small island sentenced you to be prim
and tight in balance), Browser called up words
like *julep* and *juniper* and *blubber* to command, asked Miss G.
to say her piece again in the accents of a Zola
book the school had banned, a hint he was bursting to declare
hell and black passion from way beyond Latin and Shakespeare.

4

Once upon a time, long ago, not so long ago, tomorrow –
when the heat was upon you and you wanted it all,
a bitch a slut of any sex wearing luck and brazenness
like a disguise in the new setting (prickled
by the devout who, in departing the island, put fire
to their homes, dowsed their language
to prohibit return . . .) – But no one wants stories
like this except, at best, to humour you.
The one about boarding that '60s train billed
to last a decade, though they didn't tell you that,
till the sound of *Corrina Corrina* trailed off
as revellers slipped out along the way – this tale
is too well mourned by those who were barely there.
Left alone on a train slowly filling with threat,
as if spilling from your own reading matter:
daughters too tempting, unlike those you wished
to have; daughters, revolting, like those you feared
to have, and large, slow-moving boys reopening the question
of evolution. They are here to blast your train
in slogans from the revolution you no longer trust,
like your crowd, to age gracefully
(Dylan's Corrina has grown up and Dido's impossible
son has replaced Dido's impossible husband).
Ashamed of mess, for this too-much like home,
you find yourself holding brush & pan,
working through the blame alphabet, the 'L's'
today – Lennon, Lumumba . . .

facing a partner you've never partnered, no whys
& whens, bucket & pail in the wake of children
righting the world, too busy to clean themselves:
your penance (for being too long on the train)
is empty bottles, broken glass & used clothes;
you wash and mend the furniture, pay the bills
and repair damage to the neighbours. This man
discovering this woman at a better place might draw comfort
from old books, sermons, jokes revealing
sluts and bitches to selves you can live with.
But it's too soon to indulge what might have been,
to bore with *Once Upon a Time* . . . to play this scene . . .

    5

No use complaining Dido was the prize
that slipped through fingers clutching
even now at second lives; for we are at the age
where it pays to be content, and Geraldine, intact,
her breast dry of tears, has taken to growing pumpkins
after the ball. (She protests
that this storing of her memory in attic
parts of the Great House not built
is evidence of self-abuse concealing rape.) Point
taken. And if she's a widow now we can't
be suitors, can't go on playing at being boys,
though as Maurice V., still the brightest, even though
the stroke was cruel to his profile, says:
what else are we, grey hairs and limbs too stiff
to hold small lives together, qualified for?
To enjoy this age of restoration, King back in palace,
gadgets unknown to any monarch
before our time, pets dining from luxury
of imported tins; we're kept sane by call them Court Jesters
shaming us to laugh out loud at jokes
dressed in our own disabilities: I lisp I snail, the world
grows silent; we can't eat what we like because mothers,

refusing to stay dead, don doctors' coats and frighten us
with something less spiteful than the devil.
'. . . I'm writing to you from a place called home.
Yesterday, we chased a butterfly that had hurt
itself: our debate to kill or not delicate as Chekhov. . .'
But off-stage, the spoils of conquest are women and boys
who lightly bear our names, prolonging some outdoor sport
to amuse the crowd: *There she goes! Over the bulwark*
into the sea. 'The life, the life', from an oldboy
never privileged to be 'Village Idiot' in our time,
and took a different route to manhood, his scars benign now
like cared-for flesh, suggesting fresh vegetables in the ground,
unpolluted waters and no need to seek reparations
from this State, that partner: in this stage of bliss
the grass is green is green is green and questions
of why we settle into these parts
avoiding the secret heart of hearts
the places where we, as it were, do our farts,
are never answered. If, as they say, the lessening
of one faculty sharpens another, let's pretend
that little skeletons under the crocuses, too small
to disturb sleep except in gentle questionmarks,
cloud our waking – like that shadow on that leaf,
slowly stretching out a wing to moth the garden,
leaf and moth filling some of your gaps today
all these translated years since Sychaeus . . .
And Dido herself, splendidly beautiful . . .
And Dido herself, splendidly beautiful.

A Hundred Lines

1–20

'Something is broken inside my head'
Would be a good far-off line to end with
Though when I got there the damage might have spread
Though when I got there the damage might have spread
And the rest of me not know it.
Another false start, this, to the journey. 'I must not cheat'
Is what brings me here, perhaps,
Set by an absent Master to fill pages
Till my nature blots the message
And wears it like a palmprint, reassuring,
Like others at a glance, yet darkly yours.
What have I learnt by repetition: I must not cheat,
Except to don the costume: I must not cheat,
At times, in places where dress is likely to be inspected?
And is this comfort enough to fill
The thimble of a cynic Master's dream?
But lines in detention are not questions,
Not moral issues, just irritants
Where, 'I must not cheat. I must not talk in class',
Fall, like a cat's paw, on an indifferent page.

21–40

Lines, not sentences, he said:
So change the game and not squeeze sense
From a whim. Too clever to *J'accuse*
Men of the family who have tended to suffer early failure
Of the heart, etc. Settle for the safety
Of labourers outside mocking your fortune,
Hoes glinting, like teeth on edge, cutting corners
Like this
And this:

Inside, *patriam conservabit* (he will save the country):
Some such are sauntering towards release
While I pull at soil grown heavy: *J'accuse*
Le malheur des hommes . . . etc. Nearer home, quote an ancestor,
Old tree, old stick from fruit long eaten, who never said it:
'More than good diet is required to restore heart
To men of the family . . . I will marry. Yes, I *will* marry'.
Unconfident lines, a hundred times.
And see! My stomach is no spew of jealousy. No need to blame
The cook; to misdiagnose malice from the Home Physician
Till the voice breaks in a language not yet learnt.

41–60

In the country old women prepare
Your tin bath full of herbs and sickroom oils
To prevent your friends getting out of school ahead of you.
And now, to a later family, you cite that cause
And others, for this impotence,
Your page of pity, any man's palimpsest.
Tempt them with whiff of tarts baking in the stone oven,
Those young Sundays missed –
(You can see a messenger coming up the hill . . .
And recall an uncle's tales of abroad getting bolder)
The messenger, gone past the building, has nothing to report –
     except:
In England today 58 million items will be posted –
Who will add to this stock cluttering ground and air?
Dear Y, . . . This 58th-million-&-first item can't bear the weight of its
     time. *Imagine* it.
So tell me again, uncle, of that night in Leeds, DC, Clapham
When, outnumbered, you saved the race . . .
Come back, family, with tarts from the stone oven.
It is said in another world you became a boxer
From rudeness, and got hit in the head;
And the tin bath with oils and herbs will save you from that.

61–80

an oho

I'm lost in the forest
Of my ignorance: *oho*
Spilled the canejuice, lost the limes: *oho*
Far from *annato* tree
To make me red and childlike
(My charms of axe and calabash in vain;
Spears and bows and arrows in vain): *oho*
O *maigok*, I am naked: *oho*
Great *piyaikma*, help me!
Oho

My voice is lighter than the wind
And makes no marks on your body: *oho*
My voice is smaller than your fear
Of *maigok* and *piyaikma*: *oho*
On my breath is canejuice *oho*
Fermenting inside (   )
Like a warning (   )
'Now all the dinners are cooked;
The plates and cups washed;
The children sent to school and gone out into the world . . .' *oho*

81–100

> *lines culled from 'Chief Seattle's 1854 reply' to the offer the
> 'Great White Chief' in Washington made for a large area of
> Indian land, promising 'a reservation' for the Indian people.*

How can you buy or sell the sky, the warmth of the land? / Every
part of this earth is sacred to my people. / The perfumed flowers
are our sisters, / The deer, the horse, the great eagle, these
are our brothers. / If we sell you land, you must remember that
it is sacred; / That you must tell your children that it is sacred; /

That each ghostly reflection in the clear water of the lakes /
Tells of events and memories in the life of my people. / If we sell
you our land you must remember that the air is precious to us, /
That the air shares its spirit with all the life it supports. /
I have seen a thousand rotting buffalo on the prairie / Left by
a white man who shot them from a passing train / If the beasts
were gone, man would die from a great loneliness of spirit. /
We do not understand / When the buffalo are all slaughtered, the wild
horse tamed, / The secret corners of the forest heavy with the scent
of many men, / And the view of the ripe hills blotted by talking
wires: / There is no quiet place in the white man's cities; /
No place to hear the unfurling of leaves in spring, or the rustle
of insects' wings: / What is there to life if a man cannot hear
the lonely cry of the whippoorwill or the arguments of frogs
around a pond at night? //

The end of living and the beginning of survival.

Here We Go Again

She sat for days in the posture of prayer,
With eyes closed could see leaves returning
To the trees, birds restoring harmony to the island;
And two weeks on they say to her, we say to her:
Open your eyes and see leaves returning to the trees,
Birds restoring harmony to the island.
And she's afraid, she's afraid.

And here we are again, Brothers and Sisters . . .
Three weeks after Hugo she can hear the piano:
She knows the sounds of this house, the old days
From kitchen, from animal pound, from washing-trough,

She was part of the music that kept it safe,
And we, cut off from those sounds console her,
Accompany her: *Yeah, I just found joy* . . .

She's in shock, off her head confusing
The washing of sheets in the old house
With her daughter's laundering in the new bank:
I just found joy . . . trickle of leaves . . . Yeah . . .
We're just poor people
On this patch of ground in Harris', gathered
O Lord, on a storm-damaged morning . . . *I just found joy* . . .

Was here in '24
Was here in '28
Will be here the day Soufrière
Vomit corruption back in we face.
Will be here for the Fire, the Flood . . .
. . . *Just found joy I'm as happy as* . . .

Another week: this isle is full of noises . . .
Emergency generators coughing like birds, farting, backfiring like
    birds . . .
And the Red Cross and books in the Library
To bring harmony back to the island . . .
And Persian carpets from our walls in Highgate,
And grandparents sitting again on the front verandah
To bring harmony back to the island . . . *Just found joy* . . .

Preachers, Preachers

A grandfather's voice was mocked in this village –
(not his message, dear family, the voice, the voice).
A father's sermon corrupted by flesh
and by being filtered through a son's idiom, failed also
to release a note that the island trapped in silence.
Quarantined by sea not user-friendly, Montserrat
nailed down its speech under prim verandahs, disowned
syllables brawling in the marketplace. Ancestors brushing
up on language feared the cussing, the badword, the *cuciamout*
bowelling at intervals, flood and blitz on an erring people.
In-between times we revert to good behaviour, send sons

(and daughters, now) abroad to seek lost words
for that sudden rainbow after the storm, for the arch
of flight from a childhood house that bats made,
lost to us now, with the house. Meanwhile preachers preach
around our fears: who will unlock the old voices trapped here?
Once, in childhood, I tried to free them from twin-pillars
looming, like something from the Bible, above our house
in Harris'. I failed. Friendly bees and guineafowl
cemented them to sky, to earth, with honey, with eggs.
Here's another stone, ancestor-like, squatting like a god.
Stripped by Hugo of cover, on this road above a bridge
where the murdered woman brought fever, for months, to my nights
too long ago – the bridge from Bethel whose Methodist church
alone among the Temples survived '28 – its mouth
open, like a cave we revisit despite tamer vows,
I become its audience, willing member of the congregation.
I hear it now, the lost hymn, the muffled howl;
I hear the deep, mock-laughter so much older than us.
It woke to Hugo, rumbled a profane song
whose notes broke not just glasses and promises granted on our
    knees,
but the backs of homes and churches, the order of our lives.

He was there, too, this clone, Preacher, when the rock said:
'To obey is better than sacrifice.' The man's hands are still red.
'. . . If gold and silver have to be tried by fire,
what say you to your soul which is more precious
than silver and gold?' He keeps the storm going,
three weeks late, this conduit to heaven and back, butchering
on his doorstep today, a lamb to shore up imagery.
This squat, sculptured, riot of muscle, this triumph
of pork, this Abraham confessing to be Bride of Christ,
is conscience given licence at times like this.
Other voices – party-politricks, details
of rematch between science and *myth*, the relabelling
of churches, banks – pale in description of our nakedness.
The soft pornographers, likewise, multi-
disciplined new men of travel and finesse, good
with the children, intimate spouses, clever, playful,
tuneful: SUCH BIG ERUPTIONS, GIRLS AWAKEN
NO QUESTIONS ASKED BUT PRISONERS TAKEN . . . fail
to fill the mouth left bare on the hill. They do not keep faith
with Hugo, as this stained Messenger who swaps speech
for pronouncement: 'Prepare ye the way of the Lord . . . Make
His path straight.' Already he has disciples. The island
is his parish. And those of us, uneasy, who fail to find voice
between hurricanes, must bow to the storm that blows:
'I am the Blood of the Lamb. I am the Bride of Christ.'

6

from Misapprehensions

A Death in the Family

i.m. Andrew Salkey, 1928–1995

Dear Andrew, I heard of your passing in passing,
tipping it a little in the flow of loss we must wade through
and I apologize, as we do, for not being there;
we expected you back, not like this, to those interrupted
talks in Moscow Road, which would go better now
with the strain of travel and search for allies behind us; we'd be
    wiser
now – all those Jerusalems desecrated – glossing friendship
with no sparring for advantage, no fear of surrender.

You signed off your letters, *Venceremos*. I'd planned to answer
the last one with a quip, a bit of gossip, tales
of our slippage over here. Forgive me if this sounds like a voice
grown distant; but thank you, Andrew Salkey, anthologist of
    wastes
and triumphs of our story. Ever frail but renewable, our barrier
against spoilers who make the earth more wretched, holds your
    text.

April the 28th Street

Thinking of your birthday

That way, as not to tempt fate, they pass it off
as an address. And you know how it is
with these entries in the diary, mentions
on the radio that arrest you for a minute,
as you picture a small battle fought in some distant
language, hot young men and women straggling towards the Capital,
now fêted by strangers hazy about their names,
or what they looked like, or whom they loved.

In time the street is a public square flagged
for celebration, and I, through special privilege
of the unpartnered, am transported there, re-admitted
before its gel into history, its run to ritual,
urging life back into one April partner:
and here, alone in this room, celebrate her birth.

A Diary Entry Not For Publication

So, this is day one of the life.
Off-stage, I've fought off grizzly bears
who once soiled her bed: all disreputable
ancestors will stay banished.
So, our introduction outside history
takes up years of the life.
And we survive all that. Back together,
I own up to maleness and assume the rota of men in her life.

Phew! I'm her man, her woman and something else.
Ancestors in the bathroom mirror
smudge another face till I'm grizzly
at her crying. But washed and brushed, pre-this, post-that
we return to day one of the life;
though this time round you must imagine her voice.

Reprieve

Guilty as charged: take away the bruise
on that face, humiliation by commission
on another. Add such lies of omission
as come to mind. Too smug, too smug to choose
this way out: I did in one house when we were young
ignore a cry – like spilt wine on the pavement – and read on.
    Substitute
this house for that, and a man not destitute
of imagination who stole ten years from a woman.

For reprieve I say: since then I've tracked
down part of *A la Recherche* . . . missing
from her library. So let me hurry back
upstairs (past the Guermantes' drawing-room lot) to
prevent a bruise. First, the hugs and kissing.
Then, years of putting wine back into her bottle.

These Foolish Things . . .

With you it's spring, always, in the desert,
autumn anywhere for those grown ripe
with spring; herbs of Provence in our garden
in Highgate; Basmati rice cooked just so;
nation-language: *bwoy, wha' chuppetness you talkin'?*
And maybe Louis Armstrong and Piaf for singing
telegram . . . and is that Desmond Tutu dancing the night away?
These foolish things remind me of you.

Without you, colour shrugged off the trees.
Spices from the cupboard running out
without protest. The duets mimed by extras
on the evening News show us writ large, show us grown small.
Basmati rice burnt: *bwoy, dis is no joke, eh!*
So . . . *these foolish things . . .*

At Paul and Deirdre's, Dublin

I'm not the warm knife exxing through
your butter . . . My mantra: I'm not the warm knife . . .

And now I think of lunch with friends pleased
to talk of healing things, discovering
new plants in the garden when a guest
arrives with a story she wants to tell.
But she, like you, will yield to prior
claims of garden, and promise her story with the sweet.

New thoughts of knife and butter,
and our own escape from the worst that might happen;
and wine and dinner and children served,
and everyone says yes please, let's have the sweet –
which is magical, like something tropical in the garden.
Like your pruned storybeds, sprouting again.

Turkey

That's us in Turkey with the children.
That's the family that might have been.
Who has a right to this memory, these lyric skies?
In Turkey our worlds met: East playing host
to a West you suspect of converting me.
We could live here, walking to the village
for water, food, the dust not showing up on postcards:
a villa near Fethiye, olives, yogurt etc. for lunch.

And now the villa built and lived in. Ah.
Sometimes at night I wake to Allan Poe sweat
at secrets entombed in the bedroom wall: the black cat,
screeching curses, for you, telegenic in new company.
How then to serve this sentence to life without superstition,
only memory, and a chain of logic on the imagination?

Taxis

And you know some things seem to be passed down
through the family, like being in the army
or claiming a favourite grandmother's illness:
they say, once, the ruler of a country instead of killing
people, like his father, made an enemy of the flowers;
the smell upset him. When the country was rid of blooms
he discovered what made him nauseous was new paint
applied whenever he visited a school or factory.

But taxis were the things to bring tears
to our eyes. When her first driver smiled
and he had bad teeth, she felt cheated,
like flying to America in a second class train
with waitress service. The last time she cried in a taxi
was the night a man wanted to share, and she said no.

A Story

*Angela Carter was asked for an example of a modern fairy
tale. And she said: think of a King visiting another King
in the middle of the night, to ask for a cup of sugar . . .*

King Castine knocks on Stapleton's
door late at night for a cup of sugar.
Come in, says Stapleton: what magic
brings you to my door on the one night
in 500 years I find myself at home?
I'm King of St Caesare and know
these things by inheritance, says Castine.
Or by lottery of being King for tonight.

This is very interesting, says Stapleton:
what does it feel like being King for the night?
It feels incomplete without the sugar.
And what is sugar, pray, is it your Queen?
Yes, she is the quest of 500 years, the door
that opens when you knock. Interesting, says Stapleton.

Roses

The smell won't go away: roses, he says, roses;
and moves house and country to settle
in the South of France: this workman's cottage
will grow to respect a small ambition:
villa, pond clearing into pool, the gardener
sprigging *fosse septique* with perfumes
of the region. Visitors leave restored
hearty with the whiff of what escapes

somewhat like a woman far from the scene who, yes, curses
the unguarded moment, untenses, doesn't quite flush you
out of mind: there you are doing good works
somewhere, VSOing, losing yourself in frenzy.
It won't work, she knows, seeking to atone, to justify.
Oh, there you are again, self-renewing, sniffing roses!

Love and Death

Poets, seeming to protest too much, write
last, last poems to loved ones;
and how can I say this isn't happening when,
as now, I can't keep separate converging
lines of loss – *this is mine; this is ours.*
That afternoon at an event I walked in
without you, stripped of meaning, and joined them
commemorating the death of a friend.

And here we were, at least, growing older
with grace, one fewer on the platform
than announced. And when we stood for a minute
in remembrance, I used that trust and tried
to remagic us back in place when the world
was busy, and people not like us mourned the dead.

Mammie Columbus

He shouldn't drink wine or gargle with a cold
and traumatize the throat-muscles: doctor
follows his mother's advice even though
she hasn't read, well, Kling's *A Brief History
of Finland*. But a tussle's on for the rôle
of pioneer in this house: you shrug off
names that ash you like dandruff, toying with you.
Mammie won't now lament journeys which failed
to discover treasure in family
preachers and teachers, this one a doctor,
but not of patients. In uniform old times
might mock, she masters the digital
laundrette and a machine that scrambles eggs.
She's Columbus. Scientist. Sibelius.

Conversations at Upton Park *i*

Says the boy come to visit his mother: Ruby
was the horse and the rabbits didn't have names.
But she knew that, knows that. Loss
of memory didn't extend to things at home.
Though thirty years and more of changing shape
confused children with parents; and who knows
what's embarrassing when a boy with white hair
and his mother confess over a cup of tea?

So they would keep this amongst themselves:
if suffering was done these days on television,
some things not seen must be safe. And Ruby
and the rabbits may not have understood pain.
Yet, when he went on those trips and couldn't write, she glimpsed
his ghost, sometimes, on the television and had nightmares.

Conversations at Upton Park *ii*

The father they understood; men were like that,
though father was younger than this son now
who couldn't be believed: would the boy need
more years to grow into his inheritance?
So they talked about his brother, grown up too soon,
and out of their lives: he had been wounded, pioneering
for the family, fought a long battle for compensation
which went to his head. Of course, they called him 'Skiver'.

All sorts of things bring this back:
the way one son grows into another denying
a gap in the family, still holding out
for an award lost in the post; the way no one remembers
how all this started – with a boy
giving three fingers to the machine, a skiver that sliced leather.

A History

1956. A daughter. Conceived
the day you returned £1 to the girl
at the post office. Excess change. Her blush,
not quite champagne was a sip of something Cyprusy
as if the entrails of dead sheep and cattle
showed this house, long built on nuance,
its turn of luck. A father fearing brick
and bottle in the street, talked up futures.

Now, a woman of years unbelieving
omens. Prohibitions of dad return
faith to clay. And she's released
into life on a wing and a prayer.
Pundits pundit. Crows come to Bosnia.
Cuito. 1993. Bodies, bodies everywhere.

Conversations at Upton Park *iii*

She's padded up, ready to come in at No. 3 for West Indies.
But the gloves are a problem for fingers
All tender and arthritic. And she'll need a runner.
But other pioneers in the family faced worse
Than short-pitched bowling and sledging. Her eldest son,
You know, cleared mines in Africa: that's how he lost his leg.
So, really, it's not asking much of the rest
To make an effort and pull West Indies through.

She is confused whether we're strong or weak,
A question unanswered since uncle George came back from Panama
Without his speech. *Strong* you went for a win, *weak* you tried
To avoid defeat: was that a way to live? We're not mean-
Spirited, we don't boycott football because the rightful heir
Can't kick. Now she needs someone to follow her instructions –
     like that boy Lara.

For Brian Lara

'But he lifting up the bat too high! . . .
You can't afford to lift up the bat so high.'
'But you got to lift up the bat so high,' we say, stirring it.
Though Mammie, in TV glasses, knows what she knows
and backs her bet with a look.
And, in truth, with the quickies sulking on the boundary
some slow foolishness nearly sneak through, even though
the boy, headstrong as ever, reach his century lifting up the bat.

Is sad, but not a tragedy when your luck run out,
for no man, however brilliant, can live forever
at the crease. And as one commentator was heard to say –
not Mammie, she speak for herself – Fellow said: you have to
    careful
of some little forceripe spinner who just come on and push up
    he han',
push up he han', and then bowl you a straight ball.

A Sermon in the Basement

For there's always going to be a preacher in this family
to give us a fix. Eugene's boy, they say, is reading up on the Koran,
but that's for the next generation to sort out;
so, still, we congregate for the Castine once a year
at basecamp which we can't, as yet, abandon.
Here, in our cell – you call us terrorists? – we relearn
names from the house lost in travel: *family*, again, braced
against the hurricane of exile; even the parents brought back.

The Castine sheds the cloak of conman, an island boy
with little to offer except letters behind his name.
He comes, he reminds us, as in the old days, to sup at the table.
For despite collapse around us, and falling among thieves,
we carry the promise – in boasts and regrets – of the riches of home.
For, despite this space, we are not poor, not tired; we're nobody's
    huddled masses.

7

from A Rough Climate

The Man With the Umbrella

Not wanting to point the finger, I credit him
with suffering one of those small mishaps
which seem, at his age, hard to put a name to,

like trying to figure out how time had slid
by in the traffic; and whether it was too late now
to do something about it. Or should he be grateful

that no huge shock to the system had stopped him
in his tracks. Though maybe this was a man
less haunted by my own obsessions. I see him, then,

as coming back from the dentist, anaesthetic
beginning to wear off, so the umbrella is a sort of public
shield to balance the new gap. I look around

for other umbrellas in sympathy with this ploy.
And the one that comes into view is neatly folded:
To give him support, like a fellow sufferer

shames me slightly. 'It's stopped raining,' I say,
holding out my hand to the elements. And his smile
is not unkind. And now I am wondering if I'm wet.

Psalm 151

Blessed are those who die before birth
Removing temptation from child-killers and abusers.
Blessed are the dumb, blind and insensate
So that the abundance of this world
Won't drive them to frenzy, madness and despair:
Blessed be the Lord of such things. (For, lo, the music
Of the times is yet made by the enemy.)
Blessed, too, the ends rather than the beginnings
Relieving poor creatures of the comedy of hope: that way,
The Wise Ones say, leads to disappointment,
Which is the room prepared for you without a partner.
Blessed, then, is the God of stone
Who ignores the teasing of the leaves on call them trees,
The gratuitous green of grass, the mirage of water,
Silking along the ground, like an old temptation.

For those of us who have tasted, seen and lusted
After these things, and have lost them
And are exiled from the hope of return to that feast
Must seek out a greater God of Mutilation
Where each world serves as well as the other,
And one day in a century is too short to measure,
And eternal death is on offer without prejudice,
And Circumference and Stone and America are one.

Black Youth

D'you think it's easy for your mother,
he says, like a bully, to have so many black people
around the place; and he the blackest person in our house.

And last time when my sister was naughty,
he threatened us with Big Destructions
and Punishments Too Terrible To Name.

And he's not supposed to threaten us
even when my sister hits him in the face
because she's still violent at that age; and biting

her arm and counting her fingers wrong
when she's got all ten, is bound to make her mad.
And it's not fair when we complain

because my mother only smiles or sighs
and says he lets us call him bully because he spoils us; and yes,
it's hard having one *really* black person in our house.

It Gets Worse, My Friend

In the supermarket you lose heart
and buy something fairly wholesome
in compensation: you might yet die
of natural cause. No need, then, to dwell
on an old story told with such drama elsewhere.
And yet the drip drip of benign water
wears at foundations you thought might last.
Droplets collect and mate like early life, unnoticed,
till the end is a squiggle is a river a flood
endangering your settlement. Ah, but here I am
conjuring oceans to rinse one dark mood away.
Why is it so difficult to be casual, to bring things down
to grumbling size, like chatting with colleagues at lunch
about the photocopier. Till these, too, relapse
into PC recruits for the enemy. One, who shares my subject,
targets me for disquisitions on cricket. Another,
spurning, as we do, the queue to compromise
mouths his solidarity, like a remedial
listener, while I speak. All this, I know,
seems less urgent than the story of the wrong-
looking man shot from a car belching along a Leeds
or Leipzig street. Or of your friend's arm, wrapped
as from war-collateral in a nurseless zone near to home.

And now a small cloud over a supermarket
promises rain I'm ill-dressed for. This is my neighbourhood,
those who serve here nod in recognition. At the cheese &
meat counter we queue in our mind careful of fair-play.
The stranger, confused, will be put right. 'I'm not sure,'
I say to her, trying to hint at an old arrangement,
'how they do it here.' And then someone, in secure
possession, comes to our aid, spraying cold water

on my years of teaching children in this city
how to renounce cliché. Her smile is understanding
and long-generationed. 'I think they line up,' she slips
so lightly out of idiom, 'behind the one in front.'

Hurricane, Volcano, Mass Flight

The five eggs in the dining-room
Must be turned each day to keep them fresh.
Their dish, still unchipped
Draws the eye of visitors. If the hens

Lay today, add washed eggs
To the prize and remove the first laid
For breakfast. Remember to dust all
Glassware and wipe the surface of the cabinet.

If there's no one left for housework
Leave one of the children behind to see
To things: the horse won't live forever
And pigs and goats are things of the past.

But fruit in the garden must be picked,
Picked up; rabbits out of the hutch
Kept down; the lawn cut, yard swept.
This house of your mother's can't be protected

By priest or jumbie or De Lawrence.
So do what you can inside and out.
Someone who grew here sniffing new bread
From the kitchen or bat-droppings in the attic

(Puzzled at the great drawing-room library
Shrunk to this size, casting the world
For family out there with a memory;
Or a neighbour alive and interested)

Will guard from afar a dining-room,
Still with its layered, breakable vase, egg-
Crowned, white on blue on white which
Like the piano upstairs, has travelled far.

Two Men at the Cassava Mill

It's here in the front yard near the water-trough,
well clear of the grass where Nellie spreads
her sheets, starched white with *blu*, to dry;
two men, one in short pants, working in tandem
grinding cassava enough to kill the village.

It's a *coffin*: the woman looking down from the verandah
at ground cassava shrouding its box, under the mill,
will not give in to the fear prickling her
to leave this place *soon* with her son, still in short pants:
she shuts her eyes not to see the men in action:

Left foot on a board, on the ground, stable.
Right foot peddling, pressing down on the pole,
easing up on the pole, boy hugging man
up and down in tune with the man who feeds peeled cassava
into the throat of the wheel. He is expert

and won't soil cassava-snow piling up underneath
with gratings from his fingers.
The man has no thoughts, he is dumb.
This is the 1950s, no one will know what he thinks.
The mother will shut her eyes at this ritual of men

intimate in public. The best she can do
is freeze the boy permanently behind
this rough man from the village: *why do they work
so well together?* The boy will change from short pants,
label the suitcases, and head for England with a grudge:

he will always be second-carpenter in this scene.
No one will recognize the force of his stubbornness
Grinding the cassava grinding the cassava
behind this dumb man in protecting the village
from disaster. For the mother is reduced

to panic, and the man in front is trapped
in *folk* memory where no *sign* translates him into language,
and anything you like *You're the woman of my dreams woman of
    my dreams
Rampant and foul-mouthed, endless in America, etc.*
can be put into his mouth.

I'm writing this on a computer in England,
a boy grown out of suits, years past burying
the mother. And the man grinding the cassava
is of course dead, the village new-poisoned by ash. A volcano,
this time. And who wants, anyway, to grind cassava at a mill!

I'm writing this on a computer in England
remote from the house, no mango at the back, no grape-
vine facing the edge of Mrs Meade's land: this
could have happened anywhere; the cassava smell has gone,
and nothing colours the evening air with home

but a vast night that prevents you sleeping.
And I sense what the dumb man might have thought,
and console myself. And I indulge the image of a mother protecting
her son. Yes yes, you say: but what's this got to do
with the price of coffee in Brazil. Or murder in Kosovo?

Nearing Sixty

for Eudora Fergus

Two weeks here and time to depart. The 5 a.m.
cockerels, lurid as painting
at the start of the holiday, now stitch patterns
of sound round auditioning dogs and crickets
as if to stress some theme in this quilt of remembrance:
if they knew of your complaint, the hostess seems to say,
they'd mute this third world welcome. The illness, though,
sounds like a boast to prompt a chorus.

Nearing sixty: I imagine it in letters,
less threatening than numerals whose lack of flourish
and courtesy – like something harsh, not softly
counting – prod you to revisit stretches
of life underlived. O, for Walcott's one-sentence poem
at nearing forty, managing, in the end without bitterness
or pity, to rhyme sleep with weep. There will be a party
when the time comes. I am packed now, again,
for England, looking neither forward, as in '56,
nor backward through a life skirting comedy –
though the jokes, the jokes have gone missing!
England, then, for the *festschrift*, friends rounded up,
their forced cheerfulness making you stutter,

brave, greying heads, somehow lyric and dignified
as if saved from a wreckage. Here are the pioneers
who discovered no new land to rename
after decades of travelling. Drink, then, to the attempt,
to near-misses, and check that something which you might call
the ship's log is written up in our script.

I'm thinking sixty can't be where you disembark
with Accountants from England and German bankers
whose native thrift balloon into magic pacifics
grass skirting young bodies, or in mind-swept tuscanies
beyond Provence where my poolside prejudice
twenty-five years ago rejected, in short lines
and in narratives more indulgent such late, life-weary
resting places. For I, too, may have planted a brick
here or there and watched it grow, like unearned income, into
    villa,
casual as the thought of travelling to Australia.
(A mistake, then, to have travelled to Australia.)
I can see us standing here, drink in hand, children
of friends itching to know when duty is, in duty, done.

So it must be here, back here, the island of origin.
A Sixty in good shape, to be remembered as simply fading
and distant, not gaga and twisted into some joke-recycling life-
form due to residence abroad. Not even like uncle George
back home in the '50s, Panama and Cuba and Haiti
turning him bitter. Islands cannot sleep
in case they vanish in the night: watchdogs
will worry any bone seasoned abroad till the neighbours
flesh it new; and the story of our travels will stand
retelling. From Boston to Stockholm; PNG and the Forbidden
City, you bring relief from familiar Canada and Britain;
though the Brother who soldiered in Africa upstages you still.
Once, like a new comic, you did the rounds
seeking audience outside the rum shop or with yard Characters

under a tree, folksy, as in a Selvon story. Now home is a test:
hurricanes and volcanoes have checked our progress, exxing
out certainties: this friend, well-housed in another's home laments
life in the shelters. This stains the talk. Gone is the League Table
of advantage for those who left the island, so we prick
the bubble of our ambition – and did you hear
the one about the girl in the supermarket, her hat at an angle?
Ah, it was worth travelling the world to see that hat!
Your stories of Cervical Spondylosis from 40 years of manual
typing (or from Railway portering) maintain the post-modern note.

     II

Two weeks here and discovery, magical as Columbus.
I am calling by accident on someone of a past age.
And here she is, a girl in a dress bleached
like washday making you nostalgic, as it should.
Her face, uncreased, will be our calendar, absence
of teeth not spoiling the line. A beauty preserved.
She tells the story too perfect for a book.
Propositioned seventy years ago, she almost blushes,
by my father, she has survived the generation intact.
(She might have said yes, said yes too late.)
A found mother: no disloyalty to a mother who in winning out
must have suffered from her triumph; Wish you were here, too.
Two mothers; what luck, as if to renew my apprenticeship
as son – and this time it will be better, better.
She is like a flower ashed in the garden between Eden
and after-life. I balance flattery and apology;
(What precision of speech! 'I'm not too lonely, I listen
to the voices from the radio and the television') and recall
a dream of my sister, skipping, young, and of my grandmother
materializing as a baby yet to talk: This makes me cautious.
For my eyes are open; and this mother lives alone;
and – another thing – you can't assume that friends, scattered
on four continents, will assemble for a birthday.

The Last Letter to a Grandmother

(From Athens, with a partner; from London, without)

Not like a friend's whose last letters to a wife
litter the floor or the beach now, like wrapping,
as he probes the horizon for sign that she will come back
pre-suicide: this poetry of atonement is not for us.
Time to be naked: I have lost touch with, ah, grandchildren,
a grandmother in the way, errands for a house not lived in
these forty years, and behind that the house where ancestors grew
into spirits, the source of narrative. This is a monument
built outside a plot of history, decontaminated
by a freed people's obeah. I was clever, I was
the simpleton who took words at their value. In the beginning
was grandmother's grandmother, eighteen thirty-something, so
    much
accomplished by one birth. And the next generation, women-and-
    men
carved into awe, like Greeks before Christ, the colour
of family: Uncle Ned, a Doctor, his brother a lawyer
and the JP (which one was he? who came, twice, to England) all
    preserved
from the elements, unlike blood and muscle, in our private
    museum.
Even your teenage sibling joined the Parthenon when
on a Sunday she played the organ in the Methodist chapel. Follow
    that,
you dared me early and often. Follow that through the confusions
of England. But England was 40 years ago, a lost life.

So Athens: I look back now at the wreck of more modest hopes
for the family, swop with dawdlers at the foot of *this* monument,
modern pygmies unalarmed at their own size: no one strives
to explain the statue's missing head and arm,
or to convince us how the winged creature once flew.
So I will treat you with detachment of these Greeks chomping

through salad and souvlaki knowing that Athena –
goddess of war, goddess of fertility – and Pericles, and the other
    fellow,
whatsisname – all these alliterative grandmothers, survive their
    mountain.

And now for life in the present tense.
The present, like a revolving door that slips us inside
the foyer of a foreign hotel and out again on a familiar street,
affords relief, like day-time television,
till something you took for granted shudders and stalls,
first like an ill-kept engine, then like nerve and flesh
ouch-ing accusation at neglect of what's at hand.
These moment to moment moments challenge loyalty to the house.
Thirty years ago I watched a friend kill his father;
at the end of the play Actor led his Actress to a rented room.
I alone scoffed; I knew too well that plays were tricks
you bowed out from when the night's work was done.
(And was not killing the father premature
when father, though not lost, had to be tethered to family
before the ritual with the knife? He went by natural cause, *Oh Father
Which art in Toronto* . . . side-stepping us as always). So foolish
to prolong this affair with the past, like writing
letters to a grandmother gone to dust.

II

In case you rely on it, grandmother (you're not a patient
in hospital, or in a home on the edge of conscience), in case
you're finer now than dust, more like a cloud
and take your shape through memory, let me blow something
from the past towards where you might materialize.
I honour a contract to bring you up to date. Imagine
me, then, partnered here in Athens. Imagine Athens
and partner, new provinces to our kingdom giving home
a hinterland always promised – though our talk, uncreolized,
would not be permitted in the drawing-room at home:

this talk in Athens is beyond our range of tolerance.
We changed rooms twice today, once for privacy
then for a balcony in the sun (wrong side of Acropolis) where
   a partner
might smoke: Love ... *O, Love, O Careless Love.* How did bachelor
uncles in this family conquer the world?
Theatre of Dionysos. The Odeon of Pericles. Treasures
galore. And why are boys from the island unable to pleasure
their women? Unanswerable questions scuttle you
back to comfort: clutching at (remember?) baking
at weekends, and auctions in the animal pound
and church on Sunday. For now, oh grandmother, it's war with
   the elements.
The island, whose name you never knew, is less than it was.
We are refugees now, and most of us know it. My card says:
This is Athens. Wish you were here. The house,
though not the land, has long gone. We are the talk of the town
because our mountain, dome-shaped, now a saddle, leaks
fire and anger and chokes in white dust the rider in his
   helicopter,
the supplicant on her knees. This splatters our pride
as a settled people. What trick of family will survive it? It's late;
I've let you, again, steal another day from us. There's a woman
on the balcony sobbing into ash; and, yes, we are accused.

   III

And I explained it all away as if it were fiction.
And so I'm in another part of the country, call it
England: King's Cross (and what does the cross mean, and who
is the king?); and does the time of day allow
for a happy ending? I'm a guest
in a house damp and cabbagey, a stage-set
where a man kills a woman and hides
bits of her in the river: someone on the television
tells us how it's done, knowing the furniture here
will not slide around the room in bafflement;

and in the morning there will be breakfast with strangers.
I hide all night in a deep house as from
a hurricane. On the roof, astonishing in their beauty,
filling the sky, are mammoths, not horses, male and female, who must
    be eased
down without demolishing the house.
One false move and the beautiful objects
slide into nightmare of flesh rebelling its age –
a drip in the arm, a limb amputated, foetal granny
enduring the four-letter world of pain. In the morning –
Ah, in the morning, calm, the house intact, mammoths
in another part of town, you take an old partner
to a favourite place for breakfast, and count your luck.
For this is a game of endless chances. This is
family that lives forever – though some, like cheats,
die young. Here is another part of family, someone
on the balcony wishing to enter. In this version of the story,
there's space for her, and for her gods which will topple mine.
But you've failed to meet her where she is (a little voice says)
and the search is on (O, endless, endless game) for something lost.

Athens/Montserrat, June–July 1997

Night

Teach me, nevertheless, not to be consumed
by regret: that voice on the phone
fractured from family, wish it good health,
long life and better music than I allowed
in support. I wake from screech and flare
of traffic of another man's success and, hearing you,
forget the bafflement – left stranded
wrong side of the road – of that random woman's
preference of partner for something more obscure
than human. Stop me, then, bullying
a small talent to confine itself beneath us,
to feet, well-hidden, the colour of clay.

One luxury of talking to yourself in a world
of people is hope that no one might hear
till you get it right. Unrehearsed I say: I'm not good, true
or able to prevent, on this November night,
nineteen ninety five times late in life,
one fist surprising the promise of a face;
and in the morning somewhere a child
will be startled into adulthood. There's no one around
to mug us into logic.

And who weighs time and finds it heavy?
And who says it's mine now to carry?
(To mourn one friend and bury another
might be my detail.) Though in separate houses we watch
the evening news and envy those after *Guernica*
still young with disquiet. The voice which brings this on
fades, yes, by agreement, like the house-manager
bringing up the lights on a private play.
Outside, it's Sunday morning in a provincial
town, a day to be reclaimed for one missed early –
no telltale papers – and in the evening, dinner with friends?

A Life

Today I adjust
the favourite wall
of a lover.

The vine it supports
won't arbour us
as promised.

The old arrangement
looks odd to others,
to us;

looks like another
country
we must have known.

For the Environment

for Andrew Salkey (1928–1995)
& Martin Carter (1927–1997)

It is cold this Christmas
I have no idea what it costs
to heat me: *God have mercy.*

The corner shop in Crouch End
selling knick-knacks
is now something else. The brothers
with children to educate

have gone back to Ireland.
Here in Sheffield two bookshops
which made us welcome, have gone
taking the space for browsing.

So we must live within our means
like aged parents
in new surroundings

(And who will respond to the old
jokes: it's the buttons, man,
the buttons rattling
in the new jacket, nothing more).

And I think of Andrew and Martin gone,
that generosity of spirit buried,
Andrew and Martin gone
their literary grandchildren

hustlers below stairs
full of frenzy, full of noise
desperate to inherit the house.

And I think of island and family gone,
and the heritage of remembering
respecting those spaces
new filled with rubbish.

And I am here, standing in
committing such things to memory
while memory lasts.

Hidiot (a polemic)

(with apologies to Linton Kwesi Johnson
– and for Sani Abacha)

And now there's that other man in uniform
A bit like you fellows in uniform surrounded
(Like they fraid jumbie!) by all those men in uniform.
But, folks, we not suppose to be telling joke.
Days gone when I could come in here and say
That what we and the boys discussing is the cricket
Or whether to boycott the Australian *COONAWARRA*
Cabernet Sauvignon and the piccaninny on the jamjar;
Or whether this or that PEACE PROCESS is process to peace
Or to make the conquest and defeat look good.
But things turn bad, you know:

They killing us now, man
They killing us because we DAN-GER-OUS
They killing us because we write play (Remember time
when they used only to burn book!)
They killing us because we say: Massa, We Want Clean Water
    Fi Drink.

And we don't have no gun
And we don't have bomb
And even the words to say stop tief what we have, they tief
    from we

So you discourage and defeated
But we have a memory of rising up again
So don't think discourage and defeat going stop we
And now I look pon I-man and say (*Even though you got on bullet-*
proof TV vest today) I going surprise you

So why you do um?
Is not just me a say this: *why* you do um?

(Like me hearing Miss Mabel, again, from the days in Coderington
when she did ask that man that kill woman in the village) Why you
     do um?

So stop, na?
If you is big man already with stripe pon you arm, why you so
     foolish?
You know them say when you grow hand too long for your own
     pocket
is chop they going have to chop it off: so you not fraid?
(You say the world full a hidiot giving us all a beating: *I* say they not
     killing we so)
You say this is poppyshow, I say you is jackarse
– You say, I say . . . –

And we end up right where we begin, calling each other hidiot

8

John Lewis & Co.

A LITTLE PLAY WITH INTERLUDES

... then the tribal elders or visiting dignitaries
are seated round the table.

T. CORAGHESSAN BOYLE, *Descent of Man*

Epilogue

HERE WE ARE after all those funerals,
dressed in these clothes not meant for funerals
as we head to the house or pub relieved
that food and drink will comfort and divert us
for some time longer. But already
you've said all the things necessary
to this gathering, bringing lives up to date,
like at the outing of the evening class,
halting over a Mediterranean feast
on a damp Yorkshire night, determined
to accept on your plate only such nouns
as pronounced to the satisfaction
of the waiter. But this, perhaps, isn't about food.

So we stand here, two men and a hundred years
in England between us, waiting
and not waiting to move on, balancing
fantasy of home and return against
return and home. This is not voiced, the men
have much in common; they've missed the dinner.

Act One

The Professor, with his luggage, turns up at J. Lewis & Co. in Stoke Newington early on Boxing Day in search of a minicab. Mr Lewis emerges from the unlit inner office and agrees to take the fare. On their way to King's Cross they discover they are the same age and arrived in this country within three years of each other, in the 1950s, and lived, for a time, in the same street in Kilburn. They are both on the point of departing England – the Professor, on his way to Waterloo for Paris, his prospective new home; Mr Lewis, planning for retirement in Jamaica. On the journey they review a life of, in one case, just over 50 years, in another just under, in this country. Each is reluctant to depart without leaving his mark; both are anxious about what awaits them in what they refuse to call retirement – for Mr Lewis is anxious to gain respect, and the Professor is going to research the area before settling in. Each knows he has much in common with the other, but can't resist stressing difference. Lewis plays host to the Professor who responds with a 'French' meal. They debate issues of the day. Lewis takes the Professor to a funeral. The battle to convince takes two days.

HERE WAS this man adrift, on Boxing Day
looking into nothing at the end of the street;
and when he tried to see a face in the gloom,
was relieved it wasn't his. J. Lewis,
battered and squashed by more than a night's
bad-dreaming, was a warning less subtle
than his own. 'You're open', I said
to hint that there was someone more lost
than me, 'I'd like to go to the station'.
Too blunt, the pretence of business as usual,
with nothing at this ghost-hour stirring:
two men, left over from the normal age,
filling space, like an apology. (You're
not the woman fragrant with morning-
after welcome I always imagined.)
Lewis looked like a man who feared the worst;
I blurred my presence with a step back
towards the street, and stammered a destination.
Eyes on the bags, he trusted me to view
his wall-map of London's transport tangle.
For the Northern Line it's Liverpool Street
or King's Cross with the roadworks. Straight on, then,
to Waterloo and Paris before lunch.
In the car, the passenger-door didn't lock.

*

KING'S CROSS closed, the system down, each man makes
assumptions of what the other knows
of this town, the customer pulling rank.
For who is this old guy that long ago
settled for second best, ethnic-minored
with his collusion, for decades clinging
to a language – no, not like a baby
to the finger of its mother; that's too
fanciful and precious – rather the code
of a resistance movement long entrenched

in enemy territory. Such thoughts
bring on a rush of guilt; as from a tap
with faulty pressure you thought to manage.

*

THE SECOND breakfast was like an aside
taken literally by a member
of the audience unintimidated
by the play, egg and bacon second-best
to something promised in Paris. Let's eat,
I say, thinking of my brother's warning
long ago that the lad with dreadlocks &
spliff upstairs on the bus might be the one
to save your life from killers in this town.
Cheers to Mr Lewis, out there, mornings,
nights, auxiliary patrol of the streets
of London, confusing the enemy,
riding the threat. Better, this, than Paris.
Before the first mouthful Lewis gives praise
to the good Lord, provider of all things;
and the waiter walks away unperturbed.

*

THIS IS WHAT we call unfinished business
when the train is missed for no good reason,
and the cab-driver reparks to outwit
prowlers in uniform; he thinks of you
as having options: he could take you back
to last night's haunt and unfinished business.
He must not get away with conjuring
a tone for *that* night's unfinished business
(she was not the weeping Anna of our
Russian tale, nor I adulterous Gurov).
The bags are no less heavy than before.
A travelling library to save you, yet,

from refugeedom, books to assist
at your eulogy or with the obit
should the accident occur: a couple
of classic novels you should know, something
on Bonaparte & Company, and for work,
review of old Dante and his influence.

*

CHEZ LEWIS in a part of town I find
not threatening in daylight, a hint here
and there of the Parisian street-market:
so, hospitality Caribbean-
style will be repaid with lunch, a shopping
first as in a new language, at the foot
of *l'appartement* on rue Caulaincourt
or Lamarck or Damremont on market
day. A dish for a friend to dine out on
next year in Jamaica. I make a list:
a whiff of devilry spicens the plot.
I will think of ways not to bless the lunch.

At this edge of Newington and Hackney,
a southern presence, Greekish, Turkish
and black, outdoor shopping scents the air
welcoming you abroad today. Psssh, *pssh*,
enrol these lads not liming on the street-
corner – for today we leave prejudice
sleeping it off in a neighbour's house: so,
these lads acting out your closet drama
might well be researching Dr Johnson
and his London, a task set by the Head
of English, a woman they all fancy,
to show it's no longer smart to bully
the boy from St Kitts whose name is Boswell.

*

HIS DAUGHTER is visiting in Ipswich,
so her chair here is not empty. Different
from the ex-wife and mother of his two
inside children. I stop him pulling rank
with wife and children; I will not envy
this relic; my partner, whether ex-
or current will not be summoned to tip
the scale of privilege. Better to gaze
beyond this little scene – two veterans now
looking down from their high stools, thrilling
the children with tales of adventure abroad.
(You'll be on guitar; I'll play the keyboard.)
Let us pray, he says, as if to check me.

*

BUT WHY am I here, not back there a mile
or so away where my life could again
be lived with interest? Not fate nor ill-luck,
losing the dream-children, and their mother,
but pride and vanity; yet something still
conspires against our kind – whisper it –
daring to be special in normal times.

And I'm here on sufferance, my new role
to convince this dubious brother before
we depart an England smug about who
we are, and what we share, that there's still time
to talk amongst ourselves in this debate.
No problem about the Law & Order
thing, discipline, teaching manners to *serbs*
who play the fool; low-downs who think it's smart
to burgle and rape and deal in poison.
But agreement will be tough even here.
Hanging will be deferred till later in
the talks, though humiliation, Chinese-
style, wins through: sub-standard cells, no nonsense;

walking barefoot in the snow to trial,
and garbage-target for the crowd inflamed
as in *la Révolution Française, Oui?*
Gays will be protected, particularly
pretty women, a problem, too, for later:
little men who terrorize the house
will be put out in the bush to languish.

AGREEMENT must be reached before each man
falls out of his humour justifying
the old script. (And what to do with butchers
who leave women so much dead and mangled
meat? You have to lash them, lash them, he says.)

*

AT THE END of the session we agree
not to be described as inhabiting
someone's backyard; 'backyard' stirring private
memories in Lewis, and the 'Someone'
causing me difficulty, by the day.

Interlude

So: A PARODY of the lovers' scene
early in the affaire when the storm blows
this way and that, the morning clearing up
from the night's wreck; a lazy metaphor:
packing can be unpacked, books in question –
less evidence for the prosecution –
can be dismissed to the shelf. Here, at Lewis',
telltale bags at my feet, I won't sneak past
a scribbled note on the table. Some strange
business keeps me here. I have an hour
to disprove that one or other of us
is auditioning for the unlived life.

Act Two. After Lunch; at Lewis'

THIS IS a test, the tables turned on you,
your scene alone on the stage, no audience,
but peep-holes here and there so that your foes
could pick up ammunition they might use:
so you will be self-conscious and knowing;
you will review your search for the new home.

From this corner of Damremont and Ordener
a bus to Charles de Gaulle, a bus to the Louvre;
on the métro one change to this or that musée.

Le dixhuitième *could be a perfect place to move*
says Mme from the Agency, if the search stops
short of Barbes, long fallen into non-French rule.

Austerlitz seems a long way off, two or three stops
from la Gare du Nord, then south overnight to Cannes.
Ah, but the couchette of old times no longer rocks

with passion. Next day the autoroute to Seillans
with friends past your watering-hole at Montauroux –
another 'safe house' – and a fortnight's rest again

from cruising the joints of Pigalle and Caulaincourt
in search of an address you could say en douceur.
So rue Crapeaux is out. And what of Caulaincourt,

Master of Horse to the Emperor long ago!

*

'WHEN PEOPLE have small flats – how many square
metres? Not telling – there's no longer room
for books in thirty volumes.' Travel light
and pack the library in your head, as if
you posed no threat. Oh, village Schoolmaster!

*

OUDINOT OR *Ordener? Can't afford to lose
your way home from the métro in another lapse
of concentration; no need to grab at the loose*

*change of second best despite currency collapse
of your hopes at Sacré Cœur. Rue Junot ruled out,
even Immobilier graffiti price-mocked*

*your price. The modest height of a sixth-floor lookout
on Caulaincourt showed up your fault of vertigo;
so head down the hill to the street markets, spread out*

*like old France, on pavements not named for generals:
a walk through the harvest of field and ocean and Chef
claims rue Ordener for the community. Métro*

Jules Joffrin, sans escalator, will keep you fit.

*

THERE'S disappointment, I know, at my lack
of knowledge of higher mathematics
and inorganic chemistry, and more:
no experience of putting the facts straight
to a government Select Committee
in them places you find in South West One.
Still, he's prodding me further into guilt
with interest in Ancient Rome, like a friend
wary of the academy. I pass

on this trap to betray my long-distanced
Suetonius of the later Caesars,
or *The Secret History* of Byzantium.
But don't get me wrong trying on the street-
cred now to impress the street: did you know
that a databox in the cab adds class,
that Persian miniatures bring you luck, that
'Linda' is beautiful in Portuguese?
And have I told you about Mozambique
and my hero Comrade Samora Machel?
I'm denied my usual themes of who's up,
who's down in the small literary world
outsiders have limited interest in;
or why the six-letter words who run
the academy no longer feature
in polite conversation. Nearer home,
why do decent women you know, rampant
in the good times, now vow to sleep only
with stupid men? Ah, the times we live in!
And to the cricket: which of the great teams
of our time, Clive Lloyd's West Indies giants
of the '80s, or Steve Waugh's Australians
today was *Namba Wan*? This man who calls
himself West Indian is unmoved by this.

Lewis was not a simple man, of course;
he's hitting back at me to placate God
who must be sulking still at my failure
to pay due tribute for living fear-free
in His colony: how can a man bring
argument to the truth of Matthew V:
3.11? He just couldn't understand my
beatitude. Still, we have much to prove.
The tidiness of his room is a trick,
bachelorhood less an explanation
than someone already packed for the trip.
I would be uneasy to let him see

my chaos of paper, books, printed junk
that a library now pays a pittance for:
would he eat off my plates first checking them
for dust? I must revise my view of him
as countryman not wanting to go out
to dinner. *Blackman Against Restaurants*
For Spitting in his Food. He's a solid
flesh-and-blood Man posing some obscure test,
to find me wanting. He'll come to dinner
Mondays only, with Audrey there to help
arrange the flat. That's foolishness enough
about one oldtimer in East London.

*

'I USED TO do building with a Irishman
and two other fella, they was all right.
But I knew that wasn't the job for me.'
I'm trying, still, to capture from his voice
what I may have misread of his story.
A shrewd lad, young Lewis soon left the job
as working outside, winters, in the rain
didn't suit a man used to having the sun
on his back. But his quarrel was not with
the building trade; he got transferred *inside*
decorating and painting, and in time
making the furniture, till he became
too expensive for the worthless people
who now lived in houses – a guarded joke.
(Was there a hint, a whiff of racism
that kept him outside in the snow longer
than others of the crew? So we must flick
through these mind-jottings, which refuse to fade.)

*

THIS IS after-dinner time for TV,
old films we agree on, not being family;
and sport – *Arsenal Arsenal* – Vieira
trained on the pitch at Milan the hard way.
Cheers to Patrick's mother, surviving France,
getting the boy a pair of trainers when
he needed them. A drink to all mothers.
'No one has a mother twice in his life.'
'The calypso puts mother above wife.'
'Remember my mother who fathered me.'
'Without my mother, boy, where would I be?' . . .
Then back to review a world full of tricks.
Last night, at my other place, the comics
were less funny than we remembered them,
threatening the tone of our own life-tuning;
but today we can ease up on the jokes.

England did not get off lightly, of course;
this was no clean house without a bloodstain
on the carpet. And the thieves in power
were not true men of God. I let it pass.
But Lewis knows a change of *them* in charge
is no answer to a problem older
than we know, the new man in Jamaica
no better than the light-skinned rascal thief
before him. So what's this English rumour
that the men on top, the Prime Minister
and his mates, will set an example soon
with dark-skinned wives and outside women
to make their point? And where will they find these
selfless sisters, I ask? A joke. A joke . . .

*

I LIE, I TELL the truth, I lie to see
which trick works best: this is not a woman
you're snaring for the life, so the method
is the thing; and I'm a professional
in this part long scripted: what do I do?
Well then, I write, I teach, I write to keep
my sanity in a world, etcetera,
unworthy of our gifts. Of course I wince
at the youthing of the landscape each year
when autumn fills my classroom like a threat
you must resist with grace. I raise my game
until I am the talking book you drift
off to; the eccentric grand-uncle with
his *Big Issue* sheltering from the cold.
On the good days I pass as synonym
for *dictionary* with its run words.
(There was this French Marshal whose head they said
was like a badly-arranged library.)
That's what I am, when not visiting.
So it's over to you now, my old friend.

*

I GOT IT wrong: this was no minicab
send-up of the taxi-driver blather
but a challenge I must meet: so brother,
do you know about Celsius? Do your friends
understand the weatherman on TV?
Ah, not Cicero but Fisher, German Bite,
and water freezing at zero, all that.
And did you find in your books and libraries
'when did the first man know to brush his teeth?'
Enter mature student claiming his right
to put new pressure on your shelf of books.
Ah, clowning won't do in this tutorial.

Yes, we agree on the things that matter,
awkward to talk about when you're grown up:
being waved at by a stranger, in the street;
waving back to find someone behind you,
the likelier partner, like living a life
in an old Chaplin film. But here again
he upstages me: Go while you're able.
Go before they mock your strength and you wake
in the night, alone, with no one around
to give you a glass of water. Yes, sir.

*

MAROONED *on rue Picasso, Monet, Coysevox*
I've turned up late, it seems, to the City of Light,
studios ransacked, sick and cigarettes on offer.

Or lost in early time; trapped somewhere, caught-up, caught:
the Grande Armée, 1806, spread out horse-shoe-
like across the world to rumble me. I hadn't thought

to link my fate with Styria and Carinthia. So,
I wave De Particulier A Particulier
to confuse the enemy. Marshals from Iglau

in the north, Marshals to the east, then south to where
resourceful Davout and a dozen soon-to-be
Dukes and Princes of the new order make it clear

that a non-fighting man can't join this family:
the gunner Marmont and our old friend Mike Ney
(his short name, too, improved with titles) threaten me

from places called Styria and Carinthia. OK,
without warning the Armée's on a tarmacked ring
round Paris, now facing out, now the other way.

The radio's on, I know, a cause of confusion
as you wake bleary to Mugabe in the room
or to Hornby at Arsenal. Better the Australian

antics from Messers Hayden & Co. spreading gloom
on England's hopes. This, at least, is cricket. I'll clear
my head, make a cup of tea in this outside home:

on the table, a new databox for the car.

Interlude

I

J. Lewis, dressed in his funeral suit,
is my passport to this scene: so we've come
to pay tribute to someone in Barking
we don't know. Here, in a cold country,
a brother or sister can rely on
coachloads to pay their respects. One man boasts
a hundred and twenty-nine funerals
in his time, coming too thick and fast now
for comfort. He promises not to fall
like these pioneers to the cause. Instead
he will go out with the sun on his back
and the trees in bloom, and the sea wilful
and tempting like a woman you still know.
(And something to remember the old days:
Eartha Kitt singing in that voice that drove
Orson Welles wild: 'Who were you with last night?')
This man spoke the thoughts Lewis kept from me.
Lewis is his fellow Funeralist.

II

I tried to ring you from 'France' yesterday,
my old flame. Thanks, again, for Christmas Day.
I've forgotten what I wanted to say.
Just that the trip was long, the world gone grey.
Shade at our table, no sign of soleil.
I raised our placard against the small wars.
DO NOT LEAVE VALUABLES IN YOUR CAR,
DON'T WALK IN THE PARK AFTER DARK, *etc.*
And how do you fancy a funeral?
(And do they really know that fifty-six
million people died in the world this year?)

Act Three

WE SORT OF know who is to be buried.
'I don't mind, long as the person done dead.'
Just a joke among consenting strangers,
a practised statement thrown out to test you.
So who was this, er, lady gone to ground?
She was the mother of a young woman
who forgot where she came from – the pressure
of England – and tried to put her mother
into a Home: was Women's Lib to blame
for this kind of foolishness? Pressure, boy.
That's why we have to go to we own place to dead.
And now it have thing where they burning you
like cattle with foot 'n mouth and them thing.
They taking out they body-parts to sell,
then they burning you up like evidence.
If they doing that to they own people
what chance do we have to resist this thing?
That's why we welcome mediaboys like you
who can Devil Advocate in public.
Television could show them what goin' on.
(I'm the lookalike; but I didn't let on.)

*

'SO, YOU RECKON we should pay out thousands
to these refugee and what you call them,
Asylum Seekers.' A question for me,
from a man, splendid in funeral suit,
pronouncing on an issue of the day.
'Yes, I'm Pewter Stapleton,' I offer
my hand, 'I'm down from Sheffield.' I stopped short
of making a joke about travelling
on Mr Branson's trains. Or of naming
our five main rivers. 'So tell me, where's this

money going to come from?' The tone suggests
I was wise not to joke about the trains.
But which is the pocket that holds that snatch
of dialogue like an invitation
to the event? Lewis, wearing the suit,
is not on hand to prompt me through the part.
So what have I been saying, then, about
these refugees and Asylum Seekers?
'No one gave us thirty thousand pounds or
fifty thousand pounds when we came here
to this country; we had to make it, boy,
on our own, you remember, in the teeth
of KEEP BRITAIN WHITE and NO COLOUREDS, NO IRISH,
NO DOGS – and they didn't really mean it
about the Irish.' Lewis mis-timing
his entrance redoes the introductions
(I'm his good friend, he comes to deliver
a Personal Tribute as to the dead:
I'm a man of brains, a scholar who knows
his Shakespeare and can quote Martin Luther
King the way the Parson did at service
this morning; and a brother who can hold
his own with the big boys on the telly.)

So, love and black pride is what we're about.
And the sister who's gone, God bless her soul,
knew how to respect herself. A mother
like our mother. A man must be a brute
beast of the field not to love his mother.
Honour thy Father and Mother. No one
here left to teach the children that lesson:
what if the King of England had a son?
(Is a Queen it have, you know, not a King.)
If it had a King and he had a son.
But I telling you we already have one.
Boy, black people too foolish. Tell me this:
I say, if Marks and Spencer had a son

(They is man, you know: two man can't have son;
even if is auntyman, battyman,
two man can't have pickney. 'You shall not lie
with a male as with a woman; it is
an abomination'; Leviticus
18: 19.22. The Bible
can't lie.) You listening to the Brother?
The first mourner makes his point with patience:
the King's son will not refuse the kingdom;
the M & S heir inherits the shop.
(Lewis says his sons don't want the business.)

There's a fella, what's his name, from St Kitts
going be buried at Finsbury Park next week.
(Is he dead; has the brother passed away?)
The thing is never to let them out there
think the death of a black man will serve them.
So death is not the defeat we must fear,
as long as they don't burn we like cattle.
Even though I don't believe in this thing
they call an After Life, I don't want them
to burn me up like foot 'n mouth cattle.
Burial is the only way we go earn
a piece a land in this place: the people
so prejudice they are not going to want
to share it with you. Am I right or wrong?
Lewis was upset at so many jokes
at a funeral; upset at women
smoking and drinking and carrying on
as if they was in back-home liquor shop.
His own church never does do things like that.
There's some here not of the community.

*

I DIDN'T KNOW my father, says Lewis, stiff
in his suit as if visiting his home
for interview. And what does this mean, Sir,
after a funeral; what does this mean?
Married and divorced, he has outside sons,
another son, a daughter called Manda.
Women have embraced this funeralist
in private. His young daughter in Ipswich,
unlikely Amanda from her photo,
looks nothing like him: who gifted this man
an Amanda, ah, two generations
beyond him in name and looks? He's beyond
my grasp of what is credible to write.
I didn't know my father; what can he mean?
His problems with inheritance might seem
more urgent than mine; I'm hanging well down
a family tree with little interest
in root. I claim no soil to cultivate
and must pay a price. Lewis who didn't know
his father upstages me here again.

*

BILL STICKERS is innocent, we agree.
(We have done our duty to a sister.)
At another house we might raise our glass
to Make Tea Not War but here the drink drinks
are banned. What if we're at war with the place
where they making the wine? Easy for them
to put little poison in a bottle
that is your luck to bring home from the shop.
At least the rascals scrawling foolishness
on the walls don't mean what they used to mean.
Bill Stickers Is Innocent is something
you learn to smile at now and then to show
you've lived in the country long time, not like

these fellas from wherever who don't know
yet how people here like to tell their jokes.

*

OUR GOODBYES at Waterloo will escape
jokes about Napoleon's final campaign.
This is a low-key, second-best parting
wrong side of the Newington tracks, no need
to promise not to fall under the spell
of those tired old gods of food and drink.

*

HE'S PREPARED to give something back. He says:
It does still have some prejudice back there
in Jamaica; but is not the same, you know,
as we get up here. It have funny people
dere as well but no one can come tell you
to go back home; if they don't want you there
is they going have to move. Is their problem.
(And you can get fresh bread every morning.)

*

SO TELL ME my brother, what sort of thing
you do up at the university?
O, I mark, I mark papers. More papers
and then I write the references. Oh yes;
there are meetings to attend. And then more
meetings. I forgot, I forget to mention
the teaching. I can't remember if
I do the teaching thing any more.

Interlude

DEAR LEWIS, here's a postcard left over
from today's batch, might as well be honest;
number eleven on my list of people
to impress. You've dislodged a good woman
said to be sleeping with a stupid man.
So, would you prefer the village café
with tables on the *place*, or a bit more
local colour, quaint old men playing boule
in a clearing in the Cézanne painting?
Oh, why do I bring work home to the South
of France, young Napoleon not even tracked,
coming over the St Barnard, Hannibal-
like, to Marengo (June, 1800);
Dante not reviewed, your life still on hold!

So this must be where the panic-attack
comes to the rescue at night when you wake
to the sensation of space, fighting back
the old dæmons, until *you* make it safe
shuffling back, sleep-worn, to becalm the night.
It's too late, never too late to salvage
something you let go too early in life,
a friendship, a partnership, a marriage.
Into this dream of family enter
(invader from the street; who asked him in?)
a man in funeral suit, no longer
butt of your slurry of jokes, but willing
to plead common cause and the trick of age;
my new friend in these random nights of rage.

What he said was, after the funeral,
'My children does always know where I work':
J. Lewis, Evering Road, N16;
ownership of a patch above the ground.

Well then, *my* patch has its five rivers,
the Don, the Sheaf, Porter, Rivelin & . . .
yes, Loxley. Mountains and rivers gave me,
as you'd expect, thinking space. This live plot
or that of earned England is mine to dispose of:
Amanda can be added to the list.
And so we do our double act, old man,
you, lungful of Wesley and Isaac Watts,
me, writing that outside mother into
the play set in Kilburn. She'll be reading
at bedtime *A Child's History of England*
enriching the list of Edwards, Richards
and Henrys with King Lewis that Dickens
didn't live to know. As uncle to the child
I send her unholy texts not favoured
by the Sect we call a Community.
Send her, too, a set of Leonardo's
sketches of the male form; that sort of thing.

At the next funeral I will reveal
the answer to the Law & Disorder
question. Let the criminals earn a wage,
and lock them up at night, from *five* to *five*
to decriminalize our sleep. Better
than my failed attempts at wit to deprive
felons of the right to capitalize
their name and surname. *Letter to The Times?*

He's not a Nicholas Parsons talent scout,
but he's preparing me for transmission
at the airport. The Quiz-master today
is a small man from Customs and Excise,
and he will let you out of the country
if only you can talk for a minute,
y'know, on a subject of his choosing,

without repetition, deviation
or hesitation. In another booth
a man who answers Yes to John Lewis
is not recognized by his own High Street
managers. Neither man can be let out
of England till he becomes credible.

9

Why Do You Write?

Why Do You Write?

THE SHORT ANSWER to this might be expected to reveal something of the writer's circumstances at the time the question is posed; though this might lead to a sigh of reflection, a sort of discovery that might well transcend the mood of the moment. So I am only a little bit uneasy with the answers that come to mind – that one would, perhaps, like to emulate others of the past who managed to write well; or that one wants to leave some record of an individual life's experience, both the visible and the inner worlds, to show that the life (and actions) made some sort of sense. This harmonizing of the cultures of self might tempt someone 'out there', curiously, to make connection between her life and yours (his life and yours), and to situate both lives more firmly into a general human community. Great stuff.

This is, of course, to put a spin on it: for at the same time, you (you rather than one, a better fit here) – you labour under the delusion that there is something *distinctive* about you, and that this distinctiveness is a quality that others could find some empathy with, and so not hold your separateness against you. That separateness which you variously ascribe to a special relationship with the language, to becoming conscious at a particular historical moment, to the challenge of trying to make the writing articulate other aspects of the life, is like a stubborn thumbprint that might help to prove, when you are no longer around, that you existed.

But maybe this is still too removed from what really happens: that at some point in the past perhaps difficult to locate, you give yourself permission to write; that other factors – partners, friends, extended family and the economic and political climate – allow you the space to do this and to *publish*. Then you're a writer (vulgar notion, I know, to clutch at legitimacy from the accident of publication; but as a member of the Hallam writing team I daren't apologize for this weakness). But now you have something to defend, you have some sort of constituency to hold you to account. At this point you become perhaps more confident in your articulation of what you do. You are not embarrassed to talk about finding ways of giving structure, shape and sound to sensations that might be nebulous but nevertheless contribute to your nightmares as well as to moments of consolation; or of finding your voice(s), of reconciling inner and outer selves, and in turn connecting that with something 'other', *contextualizing* your experience. You might even claim a responsibility to talk on behalf of others who, like you, have been (or are in danger of becoming) un/mis/under-represented: you are properly part of the regime that answers back. But is this becoming a little reactive? It's always good to take a further break for reflection when you start thinking and talking of yourself as if you need to be defended. The reality is that one is usually neither so grand nor so terrible (though some writers are pretty terrible) for this approach to be maintained.

But let's get real – as they say: is this where most of us live as we try to keep up with the writing athletes teasing us from the podium? Those in position usually dispense wholesome advice to the rest of us. For Graham Greene (exchanging letters with V. S. Pritchett and Elizabeth Bowen, in 1948) the writer's salvation is to avoid state patronage. (Success, happily, is taken for granted.) Bertrand Russell, on the other hand, in 'How I Write', appeals to the practitioner in us. Russell published his piece in the 1950s. Russell and Greene were men of moral courage, but neither, at his respective time of writing, was out of favour with his publisher. Or struggling to find an agent. And though our own writing environment isn't the worst we can imagine – no overt state censorship, no lack of a social infrastructure of writing and reading, no cold-war-inducing pornography, etc. – the covert means of control, like economic censorship, like PC fundamentalism, like the tyranny of fashion, still tempt our patience. But who promised us an easy life?

We hang in there because it's too embarrassing to drop out, to concoct new explanations for failure: we want to go past that mirror, by chance, and surprise ourselves when we see a writer looking back at us. (That should be disturbing enough to inform the next book, or to revise the present one.) We must go on, in a spirit, perhaps, less ontological than that of Beckett's because we might not (whisper it) be overwhelmingly skilled in other ways of projecting self that others might admire? And for how much longer will we be indulged in neglecting those non-writerly chores, hinted at – oh Successful One – in Auden's poem, 'Who's Who'? But then who's going to defend that wholesome activity of matching word to feeling, thinking, aspiring, *and* to making this seem to matter? All that. Some of that.

We might learn, unexpectedly, from the experts. One of Russell's injunctions was to say everything in the smallest number of words in which it could be said clearly, (Fine. OK). Another was to 'put a comma every four words', and 'never use 'and' except at the beginning of a sentence.' (Put a comma every, four words and never, use 'and' except at, the beginning of a, sentence.) Refine this technique from *word* to *syllable* and see what you get. *Put a comma, every four words, and never use, 'and' except at, the beginning, of a sentence.* Already, you see the possibilities here for someone rhythmically-challenged – a mild stroke victim, say. Or of a poem. (We are part of the damage of the last century, after all . . .)

Why do I write? Because I am curious about my own life in a way that I don't expect others to be, and writing about it seems a relatively harmless form of self-promotion. More respectably, I am fascinated by my inherited language (indeed, by the notion of language) and would like to add my inflections to its large meaning: I'm fascinated by the privilege – which seems to me in no way schizophrenic – of being a voice somewhat different from others and at the same time one that strangers can adopt as familiar; and I write because writing helps me to discover and reveal things about myself that I would prefer, in polite company, not to have revealed. This last bit might be poor-man's therapy. But the act of writing *could* just mature into being a transferable skill – something learnt there helping you to revise other aspects of your life. And it's fun, you know, this form of self-use, when it doesn't slide and gel into abuse. So, it's always useful to remind yourself that the music of words when strung together by the right sort of composer, hints at those elusive joys of living.

Perhaps I'm talking now about a dimension of reading, as much as about writing. So let's say that's one of the reasons I write; because I like to read.

June 2002

Notes

Notes

THE NOTES are as in the original collections. As a result there is some duplication, with more than one note on De Lawrence, St. Caesare and Wesley, while Coderington and St. Caesare, for example, are not given notes on their first appearance.

New Poems

page

63 *coalpit*: i.e. for the production of charcoal. The shallow pit would be dug, two substantial logs would be laid lengthwise, the cross-pieces of green (new cut) logs would be set down, and then piled high along the length of the pit, covered with green grass and, finally, earth. The front of the pit would then be lit, and covered over with earth. If this was done in the evening, the pit would burn all night, emitting a sort of aphrodisiac aroma, and by the morning, the mound would have collapsed, the fire out, wood converted into charcoal.

Towards the End of a Century

110 *Reverends Wesley and De Lawrence*: John Wesley (1703–1791), one of the founders (with his brother Charles and George Whitefield) of Methodism.

110 *De Lawrence* Publishing Co.: purveyor, from America, of mail-order esoteric knowledge, often practised as a supplement to 'church' religion. Influenced some of the founders of Rastafarianism.

110 *Walter*: Walter Rodney (1942–1980), Guyanese historian and political activist; assassinated in Guyana.

110 *Michael*: Michael Smith (1954–1983), Jamaican dub poet, murdered in Kingston.

110 *Legba*: Papa Legba, 'crippled Haitian/Dahomean god of the threshold, of openings', said to guard the gates to the spiritual world.

110 *Dragon's Teeth*: the name of the house. The 'Dragon's Mouth'

is the 20 km channel between Venezuela and Trinidad – so named because of the many teeth-like rocky islets along it, and the strong currents which are a danger to navigation. A London magazine which draws attention to and campaigns against racist/sexist material in children's books is called 'Dragon's Teeth'. Both these geographical and political currents flow into this – perhaps Mediterranean – outpost.

Letter from Ulster

128 *St. Caesare*: imaginary island off the coast of Montserrat in the Caribbean.

129 *Pullar and Parkhouse*: in the late '50s, early '60s, England cricket selectors cast about for opening batsmen who could give solidarity to the innings. Of the two in contention here, Pullar had some success against West Indies in 1959.

132 *Comanche Cheyenne Sioux*: Horace is moving against the trend, pushing back the damage. From about AD 1600, when enough Europeans were established on the east coast of America with superior weapons, the Indians were driven westwards into the territory of westerly neighbours. The succession of great battles – between the Chippewa and the Sioux – at Mille Lacs in the 17th century; at Elk River in the 18th and at Cross Lake in 1800, have become part of our myth. In the 19th century, the buffalo gone, the pressure westwards continuing, the defeated Sioux pushed the Cheyenne (and others) further west. The Cheyenne eventually drove the Comanche back towards Mexico.

133 *Salamis* and *Zama*: the naval battle at Salamis between the Greeks and the Persians (Sept. 480 BC) led to a notable Greek victory and heavy casualties. At Zama (Oct.–Nov. 202 BC) the Second Punic War ended with Scipio Africanus overcoming the Carthaginians under Hannibal. The entire Carthaginian army of 35,000 was killed or captured, though Hannibal escaped. His infantry was semi-trained and his elephants confused by Scipio's blast of trumpets and horns along the whole length of his line. Also, by 202, Hannibal had had 16 years of continuous high command.

133 *Wir haben . . .* : we've come to an arrangement with the neighbours about the use of the garden.

133 *Hrothvitha*: 10th-century Saxon nun who wrote plays – generally with a Christian subject – in the style of Terence.

136 *Agincourt*: the Canadian town with an English pronunciation.

137 *Harbourfront*: Toronto. Certainly, the most splendidly organized poetry reading event in the west. Presided over by Greg Gatenby.

138 *tendency to walk backwards in leave-taking*: an observation first made by Dr. Richard Bradford of Portrush, in conversation.

138 *Cassique*: local ruler in the Americas during the time of conquest, often roughly treated at the hands of the Colóns and the Raleighs . . .

MAURICE V.'S DIDO

152 *Dido*: Queen of Carthage, encountered by Maurice V. in Virgil's *Aeneid*. Sychaeus is her dead husband.

152 *urbem quam statuo, vestra est: subducite naves*: the city I build is yours; haul up your ships. (*Aeneid* 1.573)

152 *St. Caesare*: French-British island off the coast of Montserrat (invented).

152 *Coderington*, not the capital of Barbuda, is the village from St. Caesare where Maurice V. and his friends, 'the *Heathens*', now at the Grammar School in Montserrat, come from. They are quite proud of their 'French' connection.

153 Maurice V.'s titles include 'Village Idiot', 'Browser', 'Heathen'.

153 *bitches in power*: the 'bitches' are likely to be men in positions of power or influence.

153 *Lady*: after the 'Lady' boats, Canadian liners which used to transport bananas from the islands in the '30s and '40s; but had passenger cabins and acquired an up-market reputation, particularly after they ceased trading.

153 *Everton*: Everton Weekes (with Frank Worrell and Clyde Walcott, the Three W's, batting geniuses for the West Indies).

153 *Sturge Park*: the main cricket ground/playing fields in Montserrat, just outside Plymouth.

153 *bulwark*: a 'book' word, beloved of Grammar School boys of the period; like 'period' and 'cohort'. Or Maurice V.'s Falstaffian 'bed-pressing' (Part 3). Although here he could claim the less coarse Virgilian intention. Cf. Dido, after the banquet with Aeneas, 'pressed her body on the couch he left'. (Or could he be showing off his 'browsing', *Henry IV Part 2* not being a set text that year?)

154 *Libya & Tyre*: Maurice V. is careful not to acknowledge that in Virgil, Dido also rejects the advances of 'Chieftains bred by the land of Africa.' (*Aeneid* IV)

154 *Hither* (nearer or Cisalpine) *Gaul*: so called by the Romans to distinguish it from Transalpine (Nether) Gaul – the greater part of modern France, Belgium, together with parts of Germany, Switzerland and the Netherlands. Here, the speaker is showing off his acquaintanceship with Caesar's *Gallic Wars*, when all he wants to say is 'Frenchman'.

154 *Last week's Irishman*: in Montserrat (and hence, in St. Caesare) many of the fishermen of the period were descendants of Irish settlers. Accidents at sea were not unknown.

154 *parsley . . . massacre*: story of an 'uncle', supposedly in Haiti, who found himself in the Dominican Republic at a bad time. Trujillo's army, tired of driving the immigrants back over the border, decided to kill them. To distinguish the French-speaking immigrants from the native Santo Dominicans, the soldiers held up sprigs of parsley to the suspects. Those who could say *perejil* (Spanish) were passed over. Those who said something approximating to *persil* (French) paid with their life. It is said that up to 30,000 died in that 'campaign' on the Massacre River (so named before the massacre) one weekend in 1937.

154 *Agnosco veteris vestigia flammae*: I recognise the signs of the old flame, of old desire (*Aeneid* IV.23)

155 *fresh & rysche*: colloquialisms (like *pouri* = thin or *pret-up* = rude, saucy); *rysche* suggests the smell emanating from you after sex.

155 *Wesley & De Lawrence*: one, perpetrator of Methodism, the other, of esoteric knowledge, often invoked when 'Church' religion failed. (See note to page 110.)

155 *dasheenman*: hint of the social hill Maurice V. has to climb.

The poor, even if 'bright' were more likely to eat dasheen, tanya and breadfruit etc. rather than imported goods, meat. This, illogically, carried a vague hint of sexual 'strength'. (Maurice V. and the 'boys', also, weren't immune from snobbery. Cf. 'beaten by some country team literal/about games' (Part 2).

155   *rumour*: In those days rumour took an evil joy
                At filling countrysides with whispers, whispers,
                Gossip of what was done, and never done
                                (*Aeneid*)

156   *devout*: not in the narrow clerical sense; perhaps nearer to the sense in which one might link American 'fundamentalism' with the ethos of Hollywood. But these are just poor people, putting fire to their homes (many cases documented in Jamaica) prior to setting out abroad; they would allow themselves no bolt hole; they couldn't afford to fail.

156   *Corrina Corrina* [and so in Dylan, but properly *Corinna Corinna* – ed.]: a Bob Dylan old favourite.

A HUNDRED LINES

160   *J'accuse/Le malheur des hommes*: Pascal, *Pensées*: 'Le malheur des hommes vient . . . qui est de ne savoir pas demeurer en repos dans une chambre'.

161   *oho*: an *oho* (or 'oho-kari') is a special mode of expression used by the *Waiwais*, an Amerindian (Guyanese) clan for official announcements, formal requests and claims. Using short, fast, firm sentences, the speaker or *oho*-opener chants what he wants to tell his counter-claimant who, at the end of each sentence answers 'oho', which can be translated as 'yes', in the sense of 'yes, I understand'. The two participants in an *oho* sit on low stools opposite each other. The questioner invites the counter claimant to take a seat, and as each sentence ends, the adversary answers with a barely audible 'oho'. During the first stage, the opener flatters the adversary by speaking disparagingly about himself, etc. An *oho* can last from one or two hours to one recorded example lasting 26 hours.

    In the present case the counter-claimant is a woman (the second halt); and when she is seen to put her case, the claimant is clearly taken aback, and on occasion declines to answer *oho*.

161   *annato tree*: the red substance from the fruit of the annato tree is applied to faces and hands of travellers through the spirit-infested forest.

161   *maigok*: an evil spirit who lives in the forest and becomes invisible when he attacks.

161   *piyaikma*: a mountain spirit, the cause of sickness, epidemics.

161   '*Now all the dinners. . .*': Virginia Woolf: *A Room of One's Own*.

161   *Chief Seattle's Reply*, though a fake, was widely believed when it surfaced, and carried conviction. It still 'feels' right, even down to the rhetorical flashes.

The Hugo Poems

On September 17th, 1989, hurricane Hugo devastated many islands in the Caribbean and parts of the North American coast. Montserrat was the most severely hit with a dozen people killed, 90% of the property damaged and vegetation destroyed, some feared, beyond recovery. Hugo joined the hurricanes of folk memory '24 & '28, as something of a war which had been overcome, one effect of which was suddenly to have generated what is now seen as a Montserratian 'school' of writing.

163   *Harris'*: (pronounced Harrises) is a village in the East of Montserrat, which was the principal family home.

164   *Preachers, Preachers*: one consequence of Hugo was the encouragement of fundamentalist kerbside preachers. Markham's father, grandfather & uncle were also preachers.

164   *cuciamout*: a soubriquet for acacia mouth.

A Rough Climate

189   *De Lawrence*: purveyor, from America, of mail-order esoteric knowledge, often practised as a supplement to 'church' religion. Influenced some of the founders of Rastafarianism.

210   *Anna . . . Gurov*: a reference to the main protagonists in the Chekhov story, *The Lady with the Dog*.

215   *Le dixhuitième*: an address near Sacré Cœur or métro Abbesses impresses your acquaintants, further down the hill towards Barbes causes them anxiety.

217   *The Secret History*: Procopius's account of the Roman Emperor Justinian and his wife Theodora's excesses in 6th-century AD Byzantium.

217   *databox*: an appendage to the dashboard, able to receive and store messages, and help you calculate the fare. On page 222, a son's Christmas present to his father.

217   *Comrade Samora Machel*: charismatic leader of Frelimo and of an independent Mozambique, died in an unexplained plane crash (at Mbuzini in South Africa's Transvaal Province) on 20 October 1986. (34 other people on board the plane were killed.)

217   *Clive Lloyd's West Indies giants*: the present Australian cricket team, the finest in the world, draws comparison with the great West Indian teams of the '70s and '80s, led by Clive Lloyd and Vivian Richards.

217   *Namba Wan*: Melanesian pidgin.

220   *badly-arranged library*: Guillaume-Marie-Anne Brune, one of the 'Marshals of Empire' (appointed by Napoleon in 1804), was a great reader but 'only retained a vague jumble of memories from his reading'. The observation was made by Marmont, another of Napoleon's Marshals.

221   *Coysevox*: Antoine Coysevox (1640–1720), who has a street, in *Le dixhuitième*, named after him, was a leading sculptor in the reign of Louis XIV. He made numerous statues for the gardens at Versailles, and did much interior decoration, including the relief of Louis XIV in the Salon de la Guerre.

221   *horse-shoe-like*: the Austrian Prince Auersperg was outwitted by Lannes and Oudinot on the bridge at Spitz over the Danube (1805). Here's a description of the shape of the army. 'The Grande Armée was now scattered in a colossal horse-shoe from Iglau in the north, east fifty miles to Brunn, south

eighty miles to Pressburg, south-west a hundred miles to the passes of Styria where Marmont was on guard, west again eighty miles to Ney in Carinthia, and two hundred more to Augereau in distant Swabia. Massena, coming up from Italy, ought to have been by this time in touch either with Ney or Marmont...' – A. G. Macdonell, *Napoleon and his Marshals* (1934; Prion, 1997 reprint).

221 *De Particulier A Particulier*: the popular flat-finder, appearing on the bookstalls on a Thursday.

221 *improved with titles*: common practice, Napoleon creating a whole new aristocracy through his military men: Augereau becoming Duke of Castiglione; Lannes, Duke of Montebello; Caulaincourt, Duke of Vicenza; and so on. Bessières, Suchet, Victor, Oudinot, Kellermann, Macdonald, Marmont, Mortier and Soult all made it to Dukedoms. The Princes included Bernadotte and Napoleon's map-reading genius, Berthier; and some like Ney, Davout and Massena were made *both* Duke and Prince. Murat (Grand Duke of Berg and Cleve, *and* King of Naples) was almost family in the promotion stakes.

221 *the Armée's on a tarmacked ring*: the entire outer ring road of Paris is named after Napoleon's generals and marshals. Starting due north we get *Berthier* into *Bessières* into *Ney*, east into *Macdonald* into *Sérurier* into *Mortier* and *Davout*. That takes us all the way south to *Soult* curling back up west by way of *Poniatowski* into *Massena* and *Kellermann*, *Jourdan*, *Brune*, *Lefebre*, *Victor* etc. And back with old friends *Suchet*, *Lannes*, *Gouvion St Cyr* and into *Berthier*.

223 *coachloads to pay their regrets*: at 'black' funerals in England, people come from far and wide to pay their respects. Invitations are unnecessary.

229 *Marengo*: the First Consul's first great victory. Napoleon, aged 31, achieved this, over the Austrians, with a little help from Lannes, Kellermann, Victor, Desaix, etc., 14 June 1800.

230 *five to five*: courtesy of Alasdair Darroch, friend from Cumbria.

Index of Titles